This Is Body Grief

life

This Is
Body Grief

MAKING PEACE WITH THE LOSS
THAT COMES WITH LIVING IN A BODY

Jayne Mattingly

PENGUIN LIFE

VIKING
An imprint of Penguin Random House LLC
1745 Broadway, New York, NY 10019
penguinrandomhouse.com

A Penguin Life Book

VIKING is a registered trademark of Penguin Random House LLC.

DESIGNED BY MEIGHAN CAVANAUGH

LIBRARY OF CONGRESS CATALOGING-IN-PUBLICATION DATA
Names: Mattingly, Jayne, author.
Title: This is body grief : making peace with the loss that comes with
living in a body / Jayne Mattingly.
Description: [New York] : Penguin Life, [2025] | Includes index.
Identifiers: LCCN 2024032670 (print) | LCCN 2024032671 (ebook) |
ISBN 9780593656792 (hardcover) | ISBN 9780593656808 (ebook)
Subjects: LCSH: Body image. | Mind and body. | Motor ability—Psychological
aspects. | Eating disorders—Patients—Psychology. | Body
size—Psychological aspects. | Grief.
Classification: LCC BF697.5.B63 M387 2025 (print) | LCC BF697.5.B63
(ebook) | DDC 306.4/613—dc23/eng/20240822
LC record available at https://lccn.loc.gov/2024032670
LC ebook record available at https://lccn.loc.gov/2024032671

Printed in the United States of America
1st Printing

The authorized representative in the EU for product safety and compliance is
Penguin Random House Ireland, Morrison Chambers, 32 Nassau Street,
Dublin D02 YH68, Ireland, https://eu-contact.penguin.ie.

For Sean, my husband

Contents

Author's Note

As you read this book, you will find detailed stories of Body Grief as experienced by humans from all walks of life. Some of these individuals have chosen to share their names and identifying characteristics, and some have chosen to change their names while still bravely sharing their stories with the world. I hope you hold these stories as close to your heart as you would your own. I have also created some composite stories using examples from my client practice. In these stories, many details have been changed, and no identifying information has been used.

You may see yourself, your friends, your family, your neighbor, your inner child, or your past self in these stories; I ask you to hold space for all these parts with kindness and compassion. Without storytelling, there is no healing. I am incredibly grateful to everybody who sat down with me and shared their hearts and their Body Grief with this community. Thank you; you are changing lives.

Introduction

Tuck, tuck, tuck and hold. Tuck, tuck, tuck and hold. Pulse, two, three, four.

There I was on a Saturday summer morning in barre class, the smell of coffee and dry shampoo in the air, pulsing and tucking my little ass and heart away.

"Oh my god!" I yelped. Out of nowhere, I could barely move. It was as if someone had superglued my feet to the ground and filled my body to the brim with liquid cement. I took a deep breath and closed my eyes, hoping it was just a wave of exhaustion. I just needed to push through it.

"Come on, stop whining," I told myself, glancing around at the other type-A white women in the studio. But then the pattern on my leggings started to blur and disappear, as if my eyes had also decided to take a time out. I waved awkwardly to the instructor by way of apology and snuck out of the studio.

Later, I chalked the experience up to exhaustion and stress. At twenty-seven, I was graduating with my master's in clinical mental health counseling while being a teaching assistant, nannying for two households, working at a therapist's office, and starting my own business. I didn't have time to question if I might be sick. Instead, I took this early departure from my workout as an excuse to get home and do some work. But as the weekend progressed, I wondered if I had pulled my neck muscles during my "piece of cake" barre class. I was in a significant amount of discomfort. Yet, as usual, I powered through.

The following Tuesday at work, this coping strategy would fail spectacularly. The thing about your body is, when it's trying to tell you something, it won't stop sending you messages until they're finally acknowledged. And unfortunately, the longer you ignore these messages, the louder and louder they often get.

Sitting at my desk in the therapist's office, I suddenly realized I couldn't move my upper body. It was just like that book I'd read when I was young, about the girl who had polio and lived in an iron lung. I felt paralyzed. Then the pain came, pain like I had never experienced before. My eyes felt as if they were being pushed out of my head, my skull felt like it was about to explode, and my spine felt like it was made of lead. Every time I blinked, my sight got blurrier.

When my boss came out of her appointment, we immediately locked eyes.

"I'm not okay," I admitted shakily. "I think something is seriously wrong with me." In an instant, she grabbed her keys, took my hand, and locked the office doors.

"We're going to the ER," she said sternly, leaving no room for argument.

I had never been to the ER as an adult, yet this would be the first of many visits. Five similar episodes later, I would receive my first official diagnosis: pseudotumor cerebri, now called idiopathic intracranial hypertension (IIH).

Intracranial hypertension is a rare neurological disorder that causes the cerebral fluid surrounding your spinal cord and brain to build up to a dangerous point. The high pressure this puts on the spine and brain can cause blurred vision, blindness, severe head pain, bruising to the brain and spinal cord, confusion, nausea and vomiting, sleep disturbances, dizziness, numbness and tingling in the hands and feet, disturbances in gait, and ringing in the ears—in other words, a litany of symptoms that matched what I was experiencing.

The doctors explained that this would be a chronic issue that would need to be closely managed by the neurology and neurosurgery teams, and that I would need to be on medication and receive routine lumbar punctures simply to be able to function day-to-day. My diagnosis led to the first of many brain surgeries, and I became a frequent guest at the hospital.

As my abilities dwindled and it became impossible to keep up with my packed, high-achieving schedule, I felt my self-worth begin to ebb away. I was confused and distraught. *How could this be happening to me?* I had my entire life ahead of me, and now I felt like I was preparing for a funeral every day. A passive sense of doom pervaded my existence. I was in mourning, but I didn't know what for.

The day I realized there was no going back to the way I used to be, I was lying on a musty, cold hospital bed, unable to function. I had gone in for an ultrasound of my inner thigh. Following my initial surgery, my thigh was swollen, hot, and causing me severe pain at the site where they had injected the catheter. The doctors were puzzled by my ongoing symptoms. As they scratched their heads, a dawning dread crept into my veins, and I felt a deep, pervasive current of sadness wash through me. A truth tugged at my heart: my situation was no longer temporary. I was devastated.

In that moment, I was experiencing what I now know as *Body Grief.*

What Is Body Grief?

Body Grief is the sense of loss and mourning that comes with living in an ever-changing body. We've all experienced it. When our body changes in ways that seem beyond our control and therefore no longer feel like our own—*this is Body Grief.* When we realize our body will never get back to how it used to be or look, and the truth of this unravels our sense of identity—*this is Body Grief.* When we feel like our bodies have betrayed us in some way—*this is Body Grief.* When we move through the world feeling uncomfortable in our own skin, knowing we might be harmed simply because of what we look like or who we love—*this is Body Grief.* Given the systems of oppression that operate in our world, this means that Body Grief can be even more intense for people in non-white, non-cis bodies; the more our body deviates from what is considered "the norm," the more pronounced the Body Grief. We will be talking about this in depth throughout this book.

Body Grief is universal, but it is also incredibly personal—as are the experiences that can thrust us into Body Grief. You get sick and are no longer able to accomplish your to-do lists or work toward fulfilling your goals. You find yourself gaining or losing weight unexpectedly, and you worry you no longer fit into the impossible, socially imposed beauty standards that hold so much power over us. You might get into an accident and lose your mobility for a while, or even permanently. You may enter perimenopause much earlier than you "planned," grieve a pregnancy that you weren't quite ready for, or grapple with the lack of options as a larger-bodied person while out shopping with friends. Perhaps a cool new restaurant opens but isn't accessible to your mobility needs, or your feelings are yet again intellectualized and diminished when you tried to open up about racial inequality in the workplace.

All of these situations—and the losses associated with them—might trigger Body Grief. These losses may be related to control or autonomy over our body and its functions, or something about our body that once gave us some sense of worth. Our body now looks, feels, and works differently. *This is not fair*, we might think, and we feel let down, perhaps even grappling with the question of *why me?* Yet each of these experiences represents a loss, and with each loss comes Body Grief.

Until now, we have had no language—and therefore no tools—for how to process the complex range of emotions that make up this experience. The reality is, our culture doesn't believe in or support our process of grief. Grief is messy. It isn't linear. It takes time—sometimes a lot of it. Many of us are taught that our value lies primarily in our ability to produce and be productive members of society. So our tendency is to shy away from any feelings of sadness, loss, and despair. Instead, we push through our pain. We muscle through. We feel we must be "brave" and "strong."

But grief does not go away simply because we don't want to feel it. Instead, when left unacknowledged and unprocessed, it starts showing up in other ways—as reactivity and anger, unregulated emotions, isolation, eating disorders, addiction, and even trauma. It also further disconnects us from our bodies, escalating our grief and pain. The cycle goes on and on.

Body Grief, as with all grief, is a layered and complex experience.

In fact, it is trifold: we are asked to hold the sadness for our loss, find respect for our body and the functions it once had, and find gratitude for how it is right now. But when we try to "fix" our Body Grief, we set ourselves up to fail. *Just eat. Love your body. You are beautiful at any size. Time heals all.* As well-meaning as these aphorisms can be, they leave zero space for the multifaceted emotional experience of Body Grief, which must be felt, fully, in order to find our peace with the body we are in.

Because the truth is, our body has not and will never be against us. Our bodies can always be trusted, and they are always on our side. What a relief to know this, right?

But trust requires reciprocity. Body Trust is a two-way street: in order to trust our bodies, our body needs to trust us to take care of it, be kind to it, and nourish it in all ways. This is a crucial component in the journey toward Body Trust—which is a journey without end.

Acknowledging and engaging with our Body Grief means connecting with all the parts of ourselves, including the ones we keep hidden, and committing to healing what hurts so we can confidently say yes to the possibility of comfort in our body. In your willingness to meet your body where it's at time and again, you can begin to healthily grieve *with* your body and embrace kindness and compassion as a vital part of the process.

Why Me?

I wanted to write this book because I know firsthand what it means to experience Body Grief. A year or so after my intracranial hypertension diagnosis, I was also diagnosed with a genetic disorder called Ehlers-Danlos syndrome (EDS). The EDS, which I'd had since birth, was unlocked by IIH. Many people go decades without a diagnosis for EDS, which can display as being super bendy and having hypermobile joints—assets that often worked in my favor as a dancer! Now it was like the puzzle pieces all came together, though my EDS started causing me much more serious issues.

As a newly disabled woman, I wasn't prepared for just *how* different my life would be moving forward. In the years that followed my diagnosis, I would undergo nineteen surgeries and countless other invasive medical procedures, receive diagnosis after diagnosis, experience loss of mobility, loss of agency, and loss of hope. My life would change in ways I could never have imagined, and that I would never have chosen for myself. And all the while, the pain of Body Grief would continue to throb in my heart, as I was forced to slow down and face the truth: there is no cure for the loss that comes with living in a changing body.

But I'd also experienced Body Grief long before my diagnoses. Having experienced early onset puberty at age nine, and grappling with the first symptoms of my as yet undiagnosed genetic disorder, I developed an eating disorder as a kid that would last until my early twenties. I can see now that restricting food, overexercising, and managing my bodily functions through laxative use were all ways I found to cope with my unnamed Body Grief around the loss of my innocence and control over my body. My body no longer felt safe.

I have seen these same themes come up time and again in my work as an eating disorder recovery coach and disability advocate. Many of my clients feel as if they are losing or have lost a part of themselves and are therefore grieving—for the loss of what they looked like, what they were able to do, and who they were in the world. In other words, they were experiencing Body Grief. As their helping professional, my job is to guide them through this grief.

As I began speaking about Body Grief in my practice, my clients, trainees, and supervisees started to use this language, too, and I slowly found myself developing a framework to help us all make sense of this journey. Over time, I realized the experience of Body Grief could be broken down into seven phases. Not everyone experiences them in a linear way. Sometimes the phases overlap, or we skip one altogether. But for most of us, the journey through Body Grief looks something like this:

1. **Dismissal:** I'm fine. No, really.

2. **Shock:** I can't believe this is happening to me.

3. **Apology:** I'm sorry my body is an inconvenience.

4. **Fault:** Something must be to blame for what is happening to me.

5. **Fight:** If I try hard enough, I can go back to the way things were.

6. **Hopelessness/Hope:** Everything is lost . . . and the only way is forward.

7. **Body Trust:** My body always has been and will always be on my side.

The seven phases outlined here reflect the natural course our mind and body take when we experience Body Grief. In this book you will learn specific strategies for how to understand and work proactively with each phase as it arises.

What You Can Expect

In this book, my hope is that you will learn how to live alongside your Body Grief, accept it as part of you, and let go of your need to control your body and begin to be with what is. In these pages, I will first show you how to name your Body Grief for what it is, and to begin to dismantle the narrative that your body has somehow turned "against you," what I call Perceived Body Betrayal. Then I will walk you through the seven phases of Body Grief, from Dismissal to Body Trust, and show you how to identify the telltale signs of each so you can move through them. Along the way, I will teach you how to forgive your body when you perceive it as having failed you—which it never does—and find new ways to cope with strategies for self-compassion and actionable steps that you can take toward acceptance of self and others as you learn how to focus on your value beyond your physical body. To help ground the teachings of this book, I've also included tools and exercises throughout, including reflection questions, affirmations, journaling prompts, and more.

In addition to my own story, I will be sharing stories from humans from various walks of life to illustrate how Body Grief is both universal and deeply personal. With the help of these narratives, we will step into the Body Grief of individuals experiencing a range of loss: miscarriage, postpartum depression, mental illness, genetic inheritances, gender dysphoria, acute allergies, disability, body image issues, racial inequity, chronic illness, medical gaslighting, cancer, aging, accidents and injuries, food allergies, chronic pain, and sexual assault. As we will learn, while the origins of our Body Grief will always be specific to us, the feelings of devastation, confusion, betrayal, and anger toward our body that accompany this journey are universal. I see it in my practice every day.

And while there is no hierarchy to suffering, a note here on privilege—which absolutely colors all our experiences of Body Grief. I may have experienced my fair share of difficulties, but I am still a white, cisgender, heterosexual, neuro-normative, straight-sized female living in the United States with a master's degree. That's a ton of privilege, and I will never know how it feels to experience the

Body Grief of racism, homophobia, or gender dysphoria—all of which inform our individual experiences of Body Grief.

Before We Begin

Now, there is no "right way" to process your Body Grief. I give you full permission to engage with it in whatever way feels safe and right for you, at whatever stage you are at in the journey. Because living with Body Grief is a process—a process that is unique to us, and that can often bring up feelings we don't want to face. After all, *change and comfort cannot and do not coexist.* This phrase was carved into my brain in graduate school, and it reminds us that pain, discomfort, and the grief that accompanies loss are all normal, healthy facets of the human experience. But I have also learned that, with awareness, acceptance, and a willingness to share our stories, ask questions, and receive support, we can find peace within our Body Grief.

The truth is, your Body Grief will not magically disappear as the result of reading this book; it may even become stronger—but so will you. When we learn to live alongside it, we are able to function with less pain and find ways to live with more ease and acceptance in our day-to-day lives.

At the beginning of my Body Grief journey, I thought that the destination was a place where I felt no pain. But then, as waves of Body Grief hit me over and over again, I realized that this would be a continuous journey. This sucked. I wanted a solution. Instead, it has been in learning how to access my Body Grief fully, feel it, name it, and claim it, that I've landed here—a place where pain is still part of my daily experience, but I can feel completely impartial to the fluctuations of my body. A state of Body Neutrality. No longer do I label what I am experiencing as "right" or "wrong," "good" or "bad."

It simply is. My job is to show my body kindness and the utmost care, however I am experiencing it.

This is what it truly means to live with our Body Grief. I will be engaged in this process for the rest of my life. And you will, too.

Ultimately, this is a book about truth, the hard truth that pain, loss, and devastating change are part and parcel of living in a body. The truth that Body Grief is truly a universal experience, and that no one is immune to it. But when all of us are able to know and name our Body Grief for what it is, we get to heal together.

This Is Body Grief

ONE

Naming Your Body Grief

⟨ ⟩

"Y ou know the drill," my nurse said. Then she slid the IV catheter into the top of my left hand with a sharp poke of a needle.
The familiar rush of saline filled my nose as she flushed the line, and
I geared up for a four-hour infusion of the antibodies that my body
could no longer produce on its own. This had been my life for the
past twelve months.

As I sat there, my thumb scrolled my social media feeds, where
my friends were busy getting on with their lives. I started cramping
and feeling nauseous. The nurse pushed more meds, but there was no
medicine for the grief that I felt watching my youth drain away in
front of my eyes. After I received my diagnosis of intracranial hypertension, and then Ehlers-Danlos syndrome, the following two and
a half years would bring loss after loss. As I traipsed from doctor's
appointment to doctor's appointment, and underwent surgery after

surgery, my friends traveled the world. As I lost my ability to drive, my peers danced at bachelorette parties. As I lost my ability to walk without assistance and lost control over my bladder, the rest of the world opened up post-pandemic and swiftly got on with getting back to normal. Sitting there attached to the IV, tears made their way down my face. *Who even was I now? What did my future hold?*

It was in asking myself these questions that I first began to name my Body Grief for what it was. With each new twist and turn of this medical journey, I was *grieving* the loss of my health, my mobility, my identity, and my dreams.

Body Grief is something we will *all* experience on some level. For some of us, it will be the result of illness or injury. For others, it may arise in response to puberty, pregnancy, menopause, or aging. Given the very narrow societal definition of what a normal body looks and performs like (more on this later), Body Grief is also there in our experiences of mental illness, neurodiversity, and disability in all its forms.

Body Grief can be overwhelming because we have not been taught how to manage its accompanying feelings. So as we begin this journey, I want us to first spend time with the concept of Body Grief itself, and the importance of naming it when we are experiencing it. The better we understand what Body Grief is, why it comes up, and how it manifests in our bodies, the better equipped we will be to navigate the big, powerful emotions that arise when our bodies are hurting, when all we want to do is disconnect from ourselves and run. This is what I will be guiding you through in this book, as we take it phase by phase.

To be very clear, it's worth repeating: this is not a book about how to "fix" your Body Grief. Grief is not something that can be fixed, only navigated. When we learn to invite Body Grief into our lives, we are able to process it in a healthy way.

We All Need to Grieve

But we can't talk about Body Grief without first talking about grief and grieving. Prior to my clinical training as a therapist, I believed that I would not grieve until I experienced the loss of a loved one. Many of us can probably relate. But the reality is, *to be human* is to experience grief, because grief is intertwined with any and all experiences of change.

Think about it: What feelings arise when we go through a transition or lose something that feels important or integral to our lives? Whether it's a new job, a move to a new city, a divorce from a long-time partner, or recovery from an addiction, regardless of the benefits these changes may elicit, they can all induce grief. We grieve for the people we used to be, for the lives we used to live, and for the futures we thought we'd have.

Grief is . . .

Feeling like the rug has been pulled out from under us.

Questioning our identity and our reality.

Wondering how we will survive without what we have lost.

Overwhelming feelings of sadness.

Being confronted with the unfairness of the world.

Wanting to hide or withdraw from the world until this is "all over."

Yet despite grief being our instinctive physical, emotional, and psychological response to loss, as a whole, society doesn't treat grief as a natural part of the human experience. Instead, it is something to be avoided, pathologized, and compartmentalized. Or, if we can afford it, we learn that grief is best dealt with behind closed therapist's doors. But this only stifles our grieving response, which in turn makes us more prone to stress, deepens our trauma, and exacerbates our emotions.

This is what can make Body Grief so much more complicated, emotionally charged, and hard to navigate. There are very few dedicated forums in which we can openly grieve a death, let alone our own loss of bodily autonomy—hence this book, where we will build the skills and resources to lean into our emotions and our communities as we rebel against common avoidant standards of bereavement. Our Body Grief is just as big of a grievance as a death in the family; the loss creates just as deep of a wound.

The thing is, grief in *all* its forms wants and needs to be felt and expressed. This is what allows us to heal. With each difficult, messy emotion that is brought to the surface, acknowledgment is how we are able to tend to our wounds.

As a kid, my parents allowed me to express my grief however I needed. When I was a baby, I quickly imprinted on my "blankies," a pair of pretty cotton-and-lace comfort blankets that began life as my crib bumper paddings. (I think I heard all current and future mothers gasp at the thought of millennial baby Jayne sleeping on her tummy—yes, tummy—with bumpers in her bed, but I turned out fine . . . or maybe I didn't . . . which is where we laugh awkwardly.) They came to be known as "little blankie" and "big blankie," and little blankie went everywhere with me. I cried, coughed, snotted, rolled around in, hugged, and adored my little blankie. I just loved how the soft lace edges felt on my cheeks. When the padding started to spill out of the inside of the blankie, I would interlace my fingers with the silky-soft fibers, almost as a meditative practice to help put me to sleep.

I was seven years old when I lost my little blankie somewhere on a trip to the Florida Keys. The loss felt insurmountable, like a weight that was too heavy to bear. I wept, sobbed, and fell to the ground, my body literally shaking as the grief overcame me. I didn't have the language for the immensity of what I was feeling, but my body's natural biological response was to forcefully grieve *in a physical expression* of a sadness that felt too big to be contained.

Can you imagine expressing grief this way as an adult? In Westernized cultures, we give children some grace when it comes to expressing their emotions in a dramatic and uncontrolled way, but by the time we are grown, and as our experiences of grief become more serious and compounded, we tend to dissociate from our grief. This is partly to protect ourselves from the sheer pain of a loss that feels too big to bear, but partly because we are taught that succumbing to our pain—whether it's physical or emotional—is a sign of weakness. And so, we smush our grief back down, blocking it out by scrolling on our phone, drinking, smoking, bingeing on Netflix and ice cream, you name it. All because we are not taught what grief is: *the body's natural physical, emotional, and psychological response to loss.*

Exercise:

THROW A TANTRUM

When was the last time you allowed yourself to feel your grief like a child? When did you last allow yourself to throw a tantrum because the world (and perhaps your body) wasn't cooperating the way you wanted it to? Tap into this moment, really feel it. What was stopping you from throwing that tantrum, and would that primal scream have made you feel more connected with your body?

Screaming and crying are neurotypical responses to grief. But once we exit childhood, we often stop allowing ourselves to emote freely and fully. So again, ask yourself: What is stopping me from throwing a tantrum, from unleashing a primal scream of grief, and how would it feel if I actually did it?

To throw a tantrum, first, name what you're feeling. For example, "I miss the size my body was before I had a child," or "I miss being able to eat whatever I want without an allergic reaction." It may be helpful to set the mood. Engaging the senses can help us loosen up, so find some music that helps you lean into the feelings that correlate with your named Body Grief.

Now, allow these feelings to bubble up in your body and be expressed in whichever way they need. Being mindful of your safety and others', cry, scream, punch a pillow, spit, scrunch your eyes closed, and clench your teeth as your seethe and shake. Lie limp on the floor as if you have no bones in your body. Refuse to get up. Feel it all without needing to follow the "rules" about what sort of emotional expression is okay.

Feel it, don't fix it.

Feel it, don't know it.

Feel it, don't explain it.

Feel it, don't analyze it.

Feel it, don't moralize it.

How Our Unprocessed
Body Grief Shows Up

All unprocessed Body Grief needs somewhere to go. If we do not name our Body Grief for what it is, it can manifest in maladaptive behaviors meant to help us cope—including body image issues, envy, comparison, anger, self-isolation, apathy, anxiety or depression, addictions, dissociation, and other self-harming behaviors.

There's no breeding ground for these unhealthy coping mechanisms quite like puberty. During puberty, our still-developing brain is beginning to grapple with the realities and injustices of the adult world, and as adolescents, we have very little control over our daily lives. Our body is also changing in ways that feel out of our control, at a time in our lives when we start to absorb societal messages about what an "attractive" adult body is supposed to look like. All of this makes us even more susceptible to developing unhealthy ways of dealing with our unprocessed Body Grief.

When my eating disorder developed, it was a *response* to the Body Grief I was experiencing due to early onset puberty—and it brought its own Body Grief. I began bleeding into my days-of-the-week undies at too young an age. I quickly outgrew my child body and was bashfully being fitted for bras when my friends didn't even know what puberty was. I remember feeling confused as to why boys would stare at me. There was no AC in our school, but their young-yet-powerful male gaze made me want to cover up even on hot September days.

At the same time, I was beginning to grapple with the first signs of my as-yet-undiagnosed genetic connective tissue illness, or what I now know was EDS. As I mentioned, the disease affects and severely compromises the connective tissue in the body, including the brain, the spinal cord, joints, muscles, organs, and the digestive system. This impacts how I move, how I feel pain, how I digest food, how I grow, and how my body feels in space and carries itself in certain positions—all of which also affect me emotionally.

Depression also runs in my family. Add in a sprinkling of undiagnosed OCD, a shit ton of anxiety, and the immense societal pressure to be thin, and you have the perfect storm for Little Jayne to develop an eating disorder to distract herself from the confusing and overwhelming feelings of Body Grief that were stirring in her.

Inside, things were chaotic, but on the outside, I seemed fine, because I had already learned that my distress caused other people to be distressed, too. As early as age five, loud noises like the vacuum being turned on would cause me so much anxiety that I would hear people in my head screaming at me. Frightened and inconsolable, I remember relaying this to my mom. Concerned, she immediately turned off the vacuum to comfort me. Looking back on this scenario with adult eyes, I am sure she was terrified: her five-year-old daughter was hearing voices. Now with my master's degree in clinical mental health counseling, I understand this was most likely my OCD showing up. But at the time, it was brushed off as me having a big imagination and being overdramatic, and eventually, I internalized these beliefs.

My little anxious mind was doing its best to self-regulate and find a comfortable homeostasis, so I began to fixate on my body. I noticed that my belly looked drastically different from my friends' after I ate. In response, I began eating less, became hyper-focused on my bathroom habits, and would beg my parents to make me brush my teeth after dinner so I wouldn't have to eat dessert. From time to time, I would go to the gym to take a spin or Pilates class with my mom, often "forgetting" to have breakfast and insisting on packing my own lunches. All of which was just my psyche doing its best to control and make sense of the chaos that was happening in my body—in other words, manage my Body Grief.

For a long time, no one noticed. Perhaps because they thought it was just a phase, or perhaps we live in a world that normalizes this kind of behavior. But I don't blame Little Jayne for developing an eating disorder. Seeking control in a body that feels completely out of control is resourceful, especially for a child.

Many times, as you will see in the stories throughout this book, our coping mechanisms are a means of harm reduction, a way to lessen our distress, no matter how maladaptive. Unacknowledged Body Grief can look like:

- Inexplicable feelings of despair, rage, anxiety, and depression
- Constantly doubting and questioning your pain
- Overworking and ignoring inner cues telling you to stop and rest
- Purchasing endless products that promise to make you feel better or "cure" you
- Numbing with substances or dieting and restriction
- Compulsively googling what is happening with your body

In the end, we are all just doing our best to get by with the resources that are available to us. My hope with this book is to give you a powerful new set of tools for working with your Body Grief in a healthier, more empowering way.

Reflection

If a lot has been coming up for you while you've been reading this, pause here and take a moment to reflect. What did puberty feel like to you? How did you grapple with the anticipation of how it would feel to be "grown-up," the physical, hormonal, and brain changes, and the popularity contests? How did this feel in your body, and what was happening emotionally for you?

"This Is Body Grief": Naming What We Are Feeling

A year after I got my period, I remember ten-year-old Jayne crying to my mom, "When will it stop? I'm so tired of all of this!" That right there was Body Grief. But it was only after having done my personal and professional work around Body Grief that I have been able to name it as such. In doing so, I have also learned something vital to this process: until we are able to fully acknowledge what we are experiencing—to say "This is Body Grief"—it will not be possible to surrender to the healing process.

Naming our Body Grief for what it is can be harder than it sounds, partly because we have not had the language with which to describe this experience until now, and partly because saying "This is Body Grief" means allowing ourselves to actually *feel* the sadness, pain, discomfort, and distress that are part and parcel of this process. Not only are these feelings deeply uncomfortable in and of themselves, but most of us have been taught—by society or by our parents—not to make a fuss. Everybody goes through puberty, right? So who are we to find the experience traumatizing? But remember: it is natural and normal to experience grief in relation to our bodily losses. It is our collective disavowal of this that allows Body Grief to flourish undetected.

When you are able to name your Body Grief, you unlock this deep emotional process and the potential for healing. Language makes things real. Only once you are able to identify what part of your life and body you are grieving, and why, can you join forces with your body in what it is experiencing. This in turn helps to foster Body Trust—and within this, no matter how much it is hurting, you and your body become allies once again.

We can say "This is Body Grief" anytime we ask:

Who am I without my ability?

Who am I without my beauty?

Who am I without my health?

Who am I without my breasts?

Who am I without my sight?

Who am I without my memory?

Who am I without my fertility?

Who am I without my sanity?

Tapping into the Ocean
of Body Awareness

Another reason it can be so challenging to name our Body Grief for what it is, is that we live in a culture where we spend most of our time in our heads. After all, this is what most of us have been taught since birth. Starting in preschool, we may be placed in time-out for showing strong emotions. We are told that logic and strategy get things done, and that thoughts are easier to control and understand than the unpredictable, ever-changing nature of our emotions. The result is a culture in which rational thinking dominates pretty much every area of life. But this way of living is exactly what severs the mind-body-spirit connection that is the hallmark of Body Trust.

When I talk about the mind-body-spirit connection, I am not asking you to question your faith or religion—I am simply pointing out that our mental, physical, and spiritual body are all connected. To break it down, our physical self speaks to our flesh, bones, blood, and organs. Our mental self is experienced through our cognition, thoughts, and feelings. And our spiritual self is the part of us that holds our dreams, our beliefs, our quirks, our values, our connections, and our true self. When honored, nourished, and given equal attention, the mind, body, and spirit quite literally work as one. You can see this at work when you feel an emotion in your body, you are able to name that emotion and communicate it to others, and that emotion also "speaks to you"—it means something to you. This might look like the feeling of joy embodied through laughter, and then translated through dance. Or it may look like the feeling of sorrow embodied as pain in the chest and translated as tears. The stronger the connection between mind, body, and spirit, the more whole we feel, and the better we can understand and process our Body Grief.

We are designed to experience the mind, body, and spirit as one. But in today's world, it is easy to forget this. With our phones at our fingertips, we are one scroll of dopamine away from that awful feeling of anxiety that just swooped in—a feeling that we experience in our body, and that also impacts us on a spiritual level. In order to keep the mind-body-spirit connection strong, therefore, we must consciously tap into what our whole self is experiencing.

In the same way, we can only heal our Body Grief through connecting to our mind (our intellect, our rational thinking, our cognitive mind), our body (our breath, our muscles, our bones, our pulse, our flesh), and our spirit (our true self). I like to imagine this connection as a vast, deep body of water, the Ocean of Body Awareness. Swimming regularly in these waters is how we keep the mind-body-spirit connection strong.

Contemplating venturing in alone might feel overwhelming, so let's test out the water and wiggle our toes a bit. To approach the Ocean of Body Awareness, begin to reflect on any meaningful experiences that have changed the way you view your body, the way you move in this world, or the way you and your body are perceived in society. Can you name any experiences, feelings, or life events past, present, or ongoing that have altered your current experience of being in your body? In fact, close the book here and take a moment to reflect on this. How does it feel in your body to connect to these experiences?

It is very normal for certain physical sensations to arise when dipping into the Ocean of Body Awareness. Whenever I engage in this practice, I might feel heart palpitations, shortness of breath, butterflies in my stomach, and tightness in my shoulders. Sometimes my head feels light, and I have to remind myself to breathe mindfully and slowly. For some of us, connecting to these experiences may feel unfamiliar, overwhelming, and even unsafe. Whatever comes up for you, remind yourself that the goal in connecting to your Body Grief is so to heal and process it fully. Anytime it gets too much, you can always tap right back out. Compassion and grace for your process is key.

As you continue to wade further and further into the Ocean of Body Awareness, you may notice that the Body Grief gets heavier, the feelings bigger. This is all normal, and it is also when the affirmations and journal prompts I will be sharing at the end of each chapter can be helpful. Anytime you feel an itch to shut down, walk away, or dissociate, I encourage you to turn to these prompts.

We Must Feel It to Heal It: Gwen's Story

According to society, having a baby is supposed to be the most joyful and fulfilling time in a person's life. But this leaves no space for the very real Body Grief that often arises in response to the bodily experience of becoming a mother, let alone the grief around loss of autonomy, privacy, identity, and sleep that can also accompany this major life transition. This is what Gwen experienced after giving birth to her son. It was only when she was finally able to say "This is Body Grief," that she discovered that feeling whatever she was feeling was necessary for her healing.

After giving birth, Gwen was exhausted, both physically and emotionally, from what was an incredibly high-risk birth. By the time her son was a year old, she was beginning to experience what she describes as a constant spiral of thoughts surrounding motherhood and her purpose. These thoughts were all connected to the loss of her previous identity as someone who had always been very social and ran her own hospitality and meeting planner business. Whenever these thoughts popped up, she perceived them as moral failings, making her less than the perfectly selfless mother she felt she needed to be:

What if my life's purpose was to have my son, and that was it?

My son deserves a better mom, and my husband deserves a better wife.

I can't keep my son safe from danger.

I should just go away.

Gwen had heard about postpartum depression, but when her doctor examined her, they asked, "Are you having thoughts about hurting the baby?" In Gwen's case, it was quite the contrary: she only had thoughts of hurting herself, since she believed *she* was the problem. So, according to the doctor, she couldn't have PPD. This denial of her inner experience compounded Gwen's unacknowledged Body Grief, and she continued to spiral.

As time went on, this became debilitating. Nothing was getting done in the house, and paranoia that something was going to happen to the baby started to take over. Before long, it felt like Gwen's life was starting to fall apart. She no longer had a social life, she couldn't keep up with chores, personal hygiene, or daily tasks, and all she could focus on was her spiraling intrusive thoughts about herself and her baby.

Thankfully, Gwen was able to find some validation for what she was experiencing in the thriving online moms community. It seemed like she wasn't the only one struggling. Eventually, she found a blog post where another new mom discussed postpartum depression in a more expansive way, explaining that this could manifest in a person's life in many different forms, not just in thoughts of harming one's baby. In the post, she even described having some of the exact thoughts and feelings that Gwen had been experiencing. Gwen felt her whole body exhale as she read this woman's words; perhaps it was "normal" to be feeling this way after all.

In that moment, Gwen was finally able to acknowledge that *this is Body Grief.* Not that she would have used these exact words, of course. Most of us have not known how to describe the complex range of feelings that accompany our experiences of bodily change and loss until now. For Gwen, this realization simply sounded more like "What I am experiencing is mental illness, and I am allowed to heal." By naming her Body Grief, a flame was ignited, and she finally began to process what she was feeling in her mind, body, and spirit.

Gwen came to terms with the fact that she needed to get help for herself and her son. But this was terrifying: Where to start? And yet, naming the problem meant she was finally allowed to feel her emotions. Slowly, things began to feel less daunting. Gwen began to talk to her friends and family. She read up on postpartum depression and joined online support groups to begin the healing process. Most important of all, she finally began to find compassion and grace for herself in her Body Grief.

It's a Process: An Introduction to the Seven Phases of Body Grief

Once we are able to say *"This is Body Grief,"* the work of moving through it becomes a process—one that is cyclical, nonlinear, and can be as painful, messy, and confronting as hell. And not to disappoint you before we've even gotten started, but remember, this book will not teach you how to fix your Body Grief. Most of us are taught that everything worth doing should have an end goal. But if I have learned anything, it's that healing is a process that we will be invited into time and again, for as long as we are living in a body. I cannot offer you a one-and-done cure for your pain and suffering. But what I can do is give you language, tools, awareness, and companionship for the journey. Wherever you are in your Body Grief, you are not alone.

Over the years, I've identified the process of Body Grief as having seven phases: Dismissal, Shock, Apology, Fault, Fight, Hopelessness/Hope, and Body Trust. I will be walking you through each of these phases, a process I have cycled through myself many, many times, both in my own life and with my clients. Let's take a closer look at each.

DISMISSAL

The first phase of Body Grief—and a phase we will likely return to throughout the Body Grief process—is Dismissal. Here, we are in denial about what is happening in our body, as it is simply too difficult to face it head-on. Being dismissed by others in our Body Grief is something everyone can relate to; for many of us, the words "You're fine, sweetie" sound all too familiar. Unfortunately, Dismissal is far too common in a culture that prizes ability and productivity. It is easier to dismiss the source of our Body Grief than to take the time to be with our body and whatever challenges it is experiencing.

SHOCK

Shock jolts us out of Dismissal when it is no longer possible for us to ignore what we are experiencing. Often triggered by a single, fleeting incident, this is the "Oh shit!" phase of the Body Grief process, and it provides a necessary—if harsh—reality check. This can feel overwhelming, and we don't stay in Shock for long, as our body will immediately seek to restore itself to balance—often with some form of dissociation. But the purpose of Shock is to force us to acknowledge and accept exactly where we are in our bodies. Only from this place are we able to move forward, get whatever help we may need, and begin to adapt to our new normal.

APOLOGY

When we are in Apology, we often find ourselves saying "I'm sorry" on our body's behalf: sorry for having needs, sorry for the inconvenience, sorry for not being normal. On the surface, Apology seems to be about shielding others from what we are experiencing. But when we chip away at it, Apology is equally about protecting us from the discomfort of our body and its needs being seen as "too much."

FAULT

In Fault, we start chasing the reason for our Body Grief: "Why is this happening to *me*?!" When we are in this phase, we become the detective, searching for the origin of our Body Grief, the ultimate goal being to find a "fix" for what we are experiencing. Fault can feel liberating at first, but playing the blame game can quickly become overwhelming, obsessive, and lonely, especially when Fault morphs into resentment, adding to the weight of our Body Grief.

FIGHT

When we are in Fight, we are very aware of the issue at hand, yet we are determined to not let our Body Grief get the better of us. In this stage, we may start dissociating, overworking, and engaging in maladaptive, harmful behaviors that we perceive as helping us power through. But not only does this leave us more susceptible to unrealistic quick fixes, it also means ignoring and/or overriding our innate bodily cues.

HOPELESSNESS/HOPE

There are times we will feel utterly Hopeless in the Body Grief process, and like we are in a dark space with no end, driven by complete and utter despair. Yes, we will be going there, because this is a natural and normal part of the grieving process, too. But I will also show you that just on the other side of Hopelessness lies Hope. In fact, Hope cannot exist without Hopelessness, as they balance each other out. In this chapter, I will be sharing specific tools to help us find glimmers of hope in times when we feel hopeless.

BODY TRUST

Body Trust is the acknowledgment that you and your body are on the same team. Rather than the end goal of Body Grief (because remember, Body Grief has no end goal—it just is), it is what helps you move through each phase. However fleetingly we might experience it, staying tethered to Body Trust can be healing in and of itself. We do this by learning to listen to our body and to trust in whatever it is experiencing, no matter how messy or painful it might be.

As we will see later on, Body Trust is innate. But it is so easy for our trust in our body to be eroded, especially if we perceive our body as having failed or as going against us. The good news is that learning to be with our Body Grief expands our capacity to stay in Body Trust. When we know how to come back to this place of attunement with our body and its needs, Body Trust becomes an ally that accompanies us as we continue on the journey.

Often, many of us find it simply too inconvenient to take the time we need to move through the messy phases of Body Grief, let alone acknowledge the distress of not being able to perform on demand. And so we ignore, deny, and push through, striving to get back to business-as-usual as quickly as possible. But what we need is compassion, grace, patience, and time to work through each phase of the Body Grief process—and only once we name our Body Grief for what it is are we able to begin.

Of course, I get how hard this is: once we say *"This is Body Grief,"* we have no option but to feel it fully. Our grief may expand and take up more space in our lives than we want. But being with our Body Grief is the only way to heal. This book is here to help you navigate the mess. That said, I encourage you to take your time with it. This is a marathon, not a sprint, and there is no right or wrong way to engage with any of this work—only what is right for you, in your body, today.

AFFIRMATIONS

"It is normal and healthy to grieve."

"It's okay not to have the answers today."

"My body is changing, and I am safe."

JOURNAL PROMPTS

Grief feels like . . .

It feels like my body has betrayed me when . . .

My body shows up for me by . . .

TWO

The Role of Perceived
Body Betrayal

M y wedding day did not turn out how I'd always pictured it. Both of my parents held me up by my spray-tanned arms as I carefully made my way down the boardwalk aisle and onto the sandy beach, where my fiancé, Sean, and our wedding party were all masked up for our COVID ceremony. Not only did I want both of my parents by my side for emotional support, I needed them for *literal* support.

In the months prior, I had undergone some of my most serious surgeries to date and begun using a rollator mobility aid. It was the exact same model my ninety-eight-year-old grandmother used. She called it "the Cadillac of walkers," but it felt anything but sporty to me. My body was also bigger than the ones society had told me I must emulate to be the perfect bride: a single-digit size, with perfectly toned arms; a flat tummy; no scars, cellulite, or stretch marks to be seen—and *certainly* no neck brace! I'd put on a brave face, but if I'm being honest, I was petrified. As a newly disabled bride, not one of the Pinterest boards I'd created or looked at reflected my experience. None. *Zero.* I had no choice but to just do it my way.

Arriving at the rustic driftwood altar, I saw everyone swaying to the Beach Boys' "God Only Knows." Sean's eyes teared up, and for a split second I forgot how much pain I was in. Waves crashed and seagulls cawed, and Gio, our little dog and ring bearer, found a cozy spot to sit in the sand next to my lace train. When I locked eyes with Sean, I saw all the pain, relief, happiness, and hope that had brought us here, and I felt it in my heart. As sappy and rom-com-y as it sounds, with an unspoken *we got this*, we really did become one in that moment. Because goddamn—neither of us had signed up for this life.

That night, as I danced with my husband—while leaning heavily on the sleek new rollator my aunt had bought me as a wedding gift (which I promptly named Pearl)—and sang at the top of my lungs with my two sisters, I was in pain. I was disabled. I was in love. I was also frightened for what was to come, while grieving what I believed this moment *should* have looked like.

As happy and hopeful as I was for my future with Sean, this sense of grief followed me as I settled into married life. I found myself grappling with a pervasive sadness and feeling of loss, mixed with confusion, denial, and disbelief. We weren't driving off into the sunset like other newlyweds. Instead, we were sitting at home waiting for the arrival of my mobility service dog, and concern for my health was always top of mind. Had we missed out on the "fun years" before we'd even gotten started, and skipped straight to the part where our lives revolved around medical bills and fears about me falling in the shower? I loved Sean so much. But nothing about our union felt sexy or romantic anymore, and my heart was broken.

Like many of us, I am a self-proclaimed doer. I placed so much worth in my ability to get things done, and to get it done well, that grieving the significant loss of abilities that accompanied my diagnosis left me feeling helpless and less-than. I could not see or feel past my pain, and I knew by now that no treatment, medicine, or therapy would fix me. All I knew was that my body would never be able to perform the way it had.

How could the body that had been my home, that I had already helped to heal from my eating disorder, have turned on me? How could it be the cause of so much fresh suffering?

My body has betrayed me, I thought.

This right here is Perceived Body Betrayal. It is the core driver of Body Grief, and what ultimately catapults all of us into a deep disconnect within our bodies and ourselves.

Believing the Lie That Your Body Has Failed You

Have you ever felt like your body is working against you? It could be as inconsequential as arriving at the beach and suddenly getting your period, or as significant as your lower back pain getting worse no matter what you do, or even your anxiety not letting up even in moments of joy. Whenever I introduce the concept of Perceived Body Betrayal in my work, there is usually a communal aha moment where everyone just gets it, because all of us have been there.

Perceived Body Betrayal is the feeling we get anytime our body changes in ways we are not able to control, does not recover fast enough from any setbacks, experiences pain, or is otherwise unable to perform on demand: that it is somehow against us. This is a maladaptive way of coping with our Body Grief; if what we are experiencing is our body's fault, then we have something concrete to blame. And so we place ourselves at war with our bodies—when what is needed is compassion, grace, and a judgment-free zone in which to heal.

As with Body Grief, Perceived Body Betrayal stems from the societal message that our productivity, looks, and abilities are the primary measure of our worth, when in reality, all bodies of all colors, shapes, sizes, and genders hold equal value, in sickness and in health, and at every life stage. But all bodies are also destined to change, age, and experience different levels of productivity over the course of a person's life. Refusing to accommodate these shifts erodes our innate Body Trust and throws us even deeper into Perceived Body Betrayal.

This is why I say *Perceived* Body Betrayal, not simply Body Betrayal. Many of us believe that our physical self is separate from our psychological and spiritual self. We often hear things like "Her body is failing her" or "His body gave up on him." And while the underlying sentiment is well-meaning, I have a big problem with the subtext.

You see, our bodies are not separate from the rest of what makes us who we are, and they are not betraying us—ever. We just perceive they are, based on how we have been told they "should" perform. Our bodies will in fact do *everything* and *anything* to find a homeostasis, that is, to find balance, to function, and to maintain itself. This is, in fact, always our bodies' number-one goal.

The thing is, sometimes the journey toward homeostasis is not pretty. In fact, it can be incredibly inconvenient, even painful. In my case, my body seeking homeostasis manifested as the swelling, rashes, failed fusions, pain, and body convulsions that were part of my Ehlers-Danlos syndrome diagnosis. For you, it may manifest as fatigue, burnout, anxiety, feeling like you can't get enough sleep, increased appetite, nightmares, or racing thoughts.

But even when it hurts, our body is always doing what it can to protect us and keep us alive. *Body Trust springs from leaning into this awareness.* All my debilitating symptoms, which required multiple surgeries to address, were ultimately ways that my body was trying to protect me. But because I had been programmed to believe that a healthy body was pain-free, worry-free, fully functioning, and always happy, I felt like my body was letting me down—when really it was simply fighting to find balance. Part of being with our Body Grief, and growing our capacity to stay in Body Trust, is remembering that our body is *always* on our side, even when it feels like the opposite.

Perceived Body Betrayal is integral to our experiences of Body Grief. But while we feel the pain and sense of disloyalty on the inside, the causes of our Perceived Body Betrayal are external. It is in fact due to cultural ideas about how a body should look, feel, and perform, which in turn are rooted in capitalist ideals about our currency as human beings, that make it feel as if our bodies are going against us when they "fail" in any capacity. Let me show you what I mean.

Hustle Culture vs. Our Humanity

We live in a culture where our body is expected to perform on de-mand. We work for companies that expect us to meet deadlines and generate profit regardless of what is happening outside of our nine-to-five. To be the "perfect" parent, we must show up to every soccer practice and dance recital, pick our kids up from school on time, double-check their homework, and manage their screen time, all while taking care of our own ever-changing needs. Layer on being on your period, going through menopause, sustaining an injury, navi-gating an unknown illness, the expectations don't lessen, they are only compounded. This can make us feel in a constant tug-of-war with our body and its changing needs.

So when it comes to what drives our Perceived Body Betrayal and disconnects us from our bodies, we have to look to our culture—and most signs point to extractive capitalism and hustle culture, which in turn have their roots in ableism (we'll get to this in a minute). Hustle culture tells us that we are only as worthy as our work and earning capacity, our ability, and our consumer power. Meanwhile, extractive capitalism has made it so that our very survival relies on our body being able to look, feel, and perform a certain way. Each feeds into the other, creating a toxic cycle. The more we hustle, the more disconnected we become from our needs, and capitalism gains another good soldier.

What makes this even more insidious is that the hierarchical nature of our capitalist structure—where only a select few have access to power, and the majority of people are expected to help them retain it—combined with the mixed messages hustle culture perpetuates about where our worth comes from, creates what sociologists term the "ideal normal." In the West, the ideal normal is male, white, cisgender, young, neurotypical, educated, thin, and well. It is no coincidence that the more closely a person's body aligns with this ideal normal, the more opportunities, wealth, and power they have access to. Take just two minutes to scroll any one of your social media feeds and you'll instantly see what I mean. Any body that does not fit this mold is automatically deemed "less-than"—and that's before we layer on any of the challenging life experiences that may trigger Body Grief.

Of course, there is no such thing as "normal" when it comes to the bodies we are in. We may share common traits and bodily functions, but every human, and every body, is unique. This is the true nature of humanity. But in a world where we are taught to aspire to the ideal normal, and where there often is no option but to hustle hard for our survival, we come to see our body more like a machine. Something that we "use"—to earn a living, to prove our worth, and to score popularity points—versus a sacred vessel that holds our blood, bones, organs, and mind, and which allows us to form connections with the outside world.

Perceived Body Betrayal kicks in when our bodies fall short of the ideal normal. When you inevitably get sick and can't make that meeting or are just too tired to be the "perfect" mom, when chronic illness means that you can't show up to work today or an injury means you need to take a week off from the gym—Perceived Body Betrayal is there to thrust you into Body Grief.

The Myth of the Pain-Free World

There is another important factor that colors our experiences of both Perceived Body Betrayal and Body Grief: the myth of a pain-free world. In many ways, our capitalist consumer culture is predicated on perpetuating this myth, that if we just work hard enough and emulate the ideal normal as much as we can, we are entitled to a pain-free, illness-free, and violence-free experience of being in our body.

When you start to look for it, the vast majority of products and services we are sold contain whispers of this promise. Every "miracle product," "wellness breakthrough," and "productivity hack" we are peddled on social media is part of this lie, no matter how well-intentioned their creators may be. But the reality is, our body is meant to break down. Pain and discomfort are synonymous with life itself. Of course, accepting that pain is inevitable—especially when this pain is the result of prejudice—is hard. Pain *hurts*. The mental and emotional pain of trauma and injustice can lead to the kind of anguish that destroys lives. But this is the nature of life.

When we are in the grips of Perceived Body Betrayal, and in turn

Body Grief, it can be easy to forget that our bodies are wise, and that they are always on our side—however society views them, and whatever pain we are in. Believing that "my body is wrong" or "my body is failing me" distances us from what is actually happening: the myth of the pain-free world shattering in front of our eyes. But this in turn can prevent us from fully feeling and healing our Body Grief. Instead, we can sit in the suck without *blaming* our body. We can think, *My body is on my side, and it is doing what it can to keep me alive—even if the side effects suck.*

As we continue to lean into this healing work, I want to remind you that our bodies are inherently worthy. And because we are all born into an unjust system, they are also all inherently political.

The "Isms":
How Privilege Drives Body Grief

Without a doubt, privilege influences our experiences of Perceived Body Betrayal and Body Grief. When we feel less-than or uncomfortable in our own skin simply because our bodies do not adhere to the ideal normal—that is, they are not white, male, able, thin, or cis-bodied enough—this is Perceived Body Betrayal at play. The level of privilege that we embody, or anything that brings us closer to the ideal normal, dictates how much access we have to the tools and support we need to heal our Body Grief. The fact you are even reading this book denotes a level of privilege, as does your ability to engage with other therapeutic practices.

Having been in various sized bodies throughout my life, I have been treated differently and given different care based on my weight. Several of my eating disorder clients would struggle to say to themselves, "I am finally healthy, I am finally eating and ready to enjoy life recovered," because even though being larger literally meant being "well," society reflected back to them that their size was a problem.

This is the multidimensional nature of Body Grief; it doesn't happen in a vacuum, it arises in a system that has opinions, and that uses power and manipulation to shape our self-image—often in the name of profit. Whole industries are built on convincing people that they must aspire to the ideal normal or they will never be happy, healthy, and loved. But this is an impossible standard to meet, as what is deemed as physically ideal in the eyes of society is based almost entirely on genetics. This is starting to feel quite Darwinistic, isn't it? Yet the further we deviate from the societal norm, the more intense our Body Grief can be.

This leads me to the importance of certain concepts that color the entire thesis of this book. I'm talking about the various "isms"—or prejudices—that we experience as a result of existing in the body we are in. They include, but are not limited to, ableism, fatphobia, ageism, racism, sexism, healthism, classism, homophobia, and transphobia. I'll be focusing on the first five in this chapter, as they are most closely linked to the specific experience of Perceived Body Betrayal—with any loss of ability or change to our weight, and as we go through the natural aging process, it can feel like our body is going against us, and as if all our problems would be solved if we could "get back to how we were." That said, all the isms impact our experiences of Body Grief—and the more isms we embody (the less we resemble the ideal normal), the more potent it can feel.

ABLEISM

There is nothing that underscores our experience of Body Grief more than ableism. Ableism is tied to the idea that your body is only worthy if it exhibits a certain degree of physical or cognitive ability. In other words, *any* and *every* body that experiences sickness, physical or developmental disability, neurodivergence, or mental illness is deemed "abnormal," even "defective," by our society.

The extent to which our society privileges nondisabled bodies is so all-pervasive that ableism is actually one of the hardest isms to spot. But it is there in hustle culture, and it is embedded in capitalism. Getting defensive and angry when being called into the conversation to learn about disability—that's ableism. When you see a person at the store being questioned about why, when they are in a wheelchair, they can still stand up to grab the cereal on the top shelf—that is ableism. Telling someone that they don't look disabled, as a compliment, when in fact they are—that's also ableism. I'll never forget the time I told someone in my neighborhood, "I'm the girl in the wheelchair, I'm sure we'll run into each other!"—to which she replied, "I'm so sorry." I smiled, because as ableist as her response was, I knew that it came from a place of ignorance. We all have so much work to do in this area, work that we will all benefit from.

On some level, many people with disabilities believe that we do not deserve to feel good in our body because our body is all wrong. For instance, this is why certain disabled people who have internalized the untruth that their bodies are defective tend to prefer person-first language when talking about disabilities: "You aren't your disability, you are so much more than that!" But calling myself a disabled person is no different than calling someone else a tall person; it is merely a descriptor that has been made "bad" by ableist beliefs. Ableism suggests that we have been betrayed by our body if it becomes disabled—when a person with a disability is still a whole, entire human whose body is working constantly on their behalf. This is where Perceived Body Betrayal can be sneaky. For example, someone could be born disabled and so never experience Body Grief surrounding a *loss* of abilities—until they step foot into a society that treats them as if their body is broken, less-than, or wrong.

As a physically disabled woman, I have experienced ableism in regard to my physical abilities, or lack thereof, being deemed inconvenient, and my "special" needs making others uncomfortable. In my day-to-day life, I am always having to consider, is there handicap parking? Is there a ramp or an elevator? Are the tables placed far enough away from each other? Is the bathroom large enough? This triggers internalized ableism: "I am too much. I am drawing too much attention to myself. Everyone is probably so annoyed with how slow I move." My internalized ableist dialogue is loud and torments me daily. But my body is not "wrong," and it has not betrayed me. This is just ableism at play.

I wasn't aware of ableism until I myself became physically disabled, and that is *because* of ableism; the nondisabled have the privilege of not noticing how hard it is to be disabled. But we don't have to be "disabled" to experience ableism. It is present anytime we believe our body *should* be operating in a particular way or feel shame for a physical lack of ability. As Judy Huemann, the mother of disability rights activism, once said, "Disability is the one family that everyone will become a part of at one point in time." She was talking about how every body is destined to age and experience injury of some kind. And yet, we immediately infantilize and marginalize anyone with any sort of a disability.

Another way we unknowingly experience or perpetuate ableism, regardless of whether we're nondisabled or not, is through *fear of contagion*. One of the core drivers of ableism, this is the fear that by acknowledging it fully, we might literally "catch" another person's sickness, suffering, or lack of ability. On my bad days, when I have lost all the color from my face, when I am confined to my wheelchair and I am visibly in pain, strangers either have a hard time seeing me or they see me as a problem to try to fix. "Have you tried essential oils?" they'll ask. Or they'll say something like "My friend's cousin's daughter has your disease. She tried cutting out all seed oils, sugar, gluten, dairy, and preservatives, while sleeping upside down like a bat in the dark. It worked for her." In other words, they refuse to really see me and my pain, because if they do, they will be confronted with the fact that one day, *they* could be *me*.

And in the medical field, ableism rings strong when doctors attempt to "fix" a disabled person, as if they are broken or defective. Disability is not something to fix—it is just that the world is not equipped for disabled people.

We will come back to ableism time and time again throughout this book. You may even notice how strong your own ableism is as you work through your Body Grief. But once you can see it, you will be able to learn from it and move forward.

FATPHOBIA/FATISM

You don't have to look very hard to see that in a fatphobic society such as ours, fat bodies are also treated as less-than or defective. Once you see it, fatphobia is everywhere: from the endless marketing of various diets and cleanses, to body-focused compliments, to calling ourselves "bad" for simply eating a cookie, to lack of accessible sizing at most stores.

Fatphobia is often hidden in concern about people's health: "She *must* be unhealthy at that size." But the research actually refutes this. Health is not just about size. Instead, according to the framework I use with my clients, health can be broken down into six pillars: social, emotional, financial, physical, nutritional, and spiritual. Our overall well-being does not come down to weight alone and instead requires a balance of all these elements. In fact, quite often weight is not simply the direct result of food intake or exercise. Genetics play a huge role in one's body size, as do hormones, socioeconomic status, education, illness, mental health, and history of dieting—essentially making basing someone's worth on their body size not only unjust, but ignorant.

This truth can be uncomfortable, because it goes against so much of what mainstream media, beauty culture, and diet culture has taught us. As an eating-disorder and body-image specialist, I have seen how these powerful, profit-driven forces keep many of us stuck in destructive cycles of self-hatred that manifest in Perceived Body Betrayal and deep Body Grief. For example, many of my clients experience Perceived Body Betrayal after their disordered eating patterns result in disrupted digestion. Unfortunately, our body reacts to what we feed it and do not feed it, no matter the circumstances, and our gastrointestinal system slows down when we don't feed it enough. This commonly leads to delayed motility, constipation, or even gastroparesis. These are not examples of our body betraying us; these conditions are directly linked to the impact of fatphobia and diet culture.

Unfortunately, the message that "fat is less-than" is so strong in our society that, much like ableism, we have all internalized a degree of fatphobia. This makes it hard to name our Body Grief. Instead, we become hypnotized by marketing messages telling us that if we go on this cleanse, we will lose X amount of weight, heal our gut, and finally be happy. Not only is this not true, it is toxic, and it plays to our internalized ableism—the notion that being in a bigger body means we are unwell or unable.

As we work through the seven stages of Body Grief, you will likely be challenged to examine your own internalized fatphobia.

This is okay! Again, the key to undoing these thoughts is bringing awareness to our biases and leaning into the discomfort of confronting them.

AGEISM

Perhaps everybody can relate to feeling betrayed by the aging process. After all, youth is closely associated with ability—and in an ageist society, being old is often seen as a disability in and of itself. We see this in rampant and largely ignored age-based discrimination, cruel and mocking cultural portrayals of older folx, and a multitrillion-dollar anti-aging industry. One reason I asked my aunt for a sleek, new rollator? Because I hated using the same one as my grandma. That's ageism right there.

Here's the truth: it is a privilege to age. It is proof that we are alive! Of course, as I've been reminded while speaking about Body Grief to people in my community age seventy and up, it is also normal to grieve who we used to be and what we used to be able to do with ease. People I've met described how no longer being able to get down on the floor and play with the grandkids felt like a betrayal, creating Perceived Body Betrayal around not being seen as the "fun" grandparent anymore. Here we see internalized ageism at work, driven by the idea that only youthful, active bodies have something valuable to contribute.

The reality is, as we age, our joints get stiff. Our bones become more brittle. It can be hard to get down onto and up from the ground. We become less sharp, less able to bounce back as quickly as we used to. This is our body's way of signaling that it is time to rest and enjoy being a safe harbor and a font of wisdom, rather than the one on the floor building forts. But through the lens of Body Trust, both sadness and acceptance can exist. When we are able to be with our Body

Grief, we are able to mourn what our body used to be able to do *and* develop an appreciation for this new life stage: a time to quit scrambling so hard and to enjoy and appreciate the life we have built.

RACISM

Racism is such an all-pervasive ism, that it is deeply interwoven with the workings of our justice system, infrastructure, and political agenda. Beginning with the genocide of the indigenous American people, the United States was built on white supremacy, while much of the wealth that this nation has generated was built on the backs of enslaved and oppressed Black and Brown people. This is crucial to understanding how Body Grief impacts people of color differently: when your body is deemed inherently less-than, the path to Body Trust becomes that much more challenging on every level.

In addition, the tenets of white supremacy exacerbate Perceived Body Betrayal in all individuals, as they uphold the concept of the ideal normal, aka white. These tenets, as defined by Kenneth Jones and Tema Okun in their book *Dismantling Racism: A Workbook for Social Change Groups*, include perfectionism, sense of urgency, defensiveness, quantity over quality, worship of the written word, paternalism, either/or thinking, power hoarding, fear of open conflict, individualism, progress is bigger and more, objectivity, and the right to comfort. The extent to which one experiences Perceived Body Betrayal is deeply tied to the prevalence of these tenets, while those healing their own Body Grief while also confronting racism and white supremacy on a daily basis have to make their way through double, triple the rubble. You'll see this dynamic illustrated in stories throughout this book.

SEXISM

French philosopher Simone de Beauvoir once said, "Man is defined as a human being and woman as a female—whenever she behaves as a human being she is said to imitate the male." This gets to the heart of how sexism works. Simply put, all female bodies are considered other or less than the male ideal normal, and are not given the same freedoms, respect, or level of safety. This discrimination extends to bodies that appear more feminine. This means that all women and woman-identifying individuals, as well as many trans and nonbinary folx, will be dealing with the impact of sexism in their experiences of Body Grief.

Sexism impacts people's experiences of both Body Grief and Perceived Body Betrayal in a myriad of ways. Not being able to breastfeed at work is because of sexism. Being reprimanded or assaulted for expressing your gender through your clothing and the way you move your body is because of sexism. Feeling afraid walking alone to your car at night is sexism, as is the fact that 91 percent of rape and sexual assault victims are female.

Another manifestation of this ism is that "women's issues" are not taken as seriously or studied as extensively by the medical industry. Take EDS for example. Most men are diagnosed 9.6 years earlier on average than women, and experience quantifiably less Perceived Body Betrayal as a result. In another example, it takes on average 10 years for a woman to be diagnosed with endometriosis—an excruciatingly painful condition in which cells from the lining of the uterus begin to grow outside of the uterus (and also part of my Body Grief journey). As an example of how racism and sexism intersect within the context of Body Grief, Black women in the United States are three times more likely than white women to die of pregnancy-related causes. This is due to lower quality healthcare overall, underlying chronic conditions, higher levels of cortisol, and implicit bias among medical professionals.

One thing to remember when considering the impact of all these isms on our Body Grief journeys is that they can only ever be enacted by people in positions of power. We will sometimes hear that sexism or racism, for example, can go "both ways," but I completely disagree, and I know many are with me on this. Power differentials mean that all isms are experienced by those who embody whatever traits are deemed less-than, by those whose bodies diverge from the ideal normal.

Reflection Questions

What have been your experiences with ableism, fatism, and ageism? And what about the other isms that you experience in your body—such as racism, homophobia, classism, and lookism? Do they ever manifest as Perceived Body Betrayal? How do you think they might have informed and exacerbated your experiences with Body Grief?

THE ISMS AT PLAY: TONY'S STORY

Identities are really just labels for the bodies we are in, yet prejudice exists in its every realm. Every ism that applies to you will impact your experience of Perceived Body Betrayal and Body Grief—beginning with your ability to see it and name it for what it is. This was the case with Tony.

The pubescent, preteen years were a weird time for everyone, with hormones and all sorts of unanswered questions about how the world works running wild. But for Tony, whose whole life growing up in the southside of Minneapolis had been written in trauma, that time was extra hard. His father was, in his own words, a "drug addict who abused women" and was murdered when Tony was just three years old. When Tony was five, his mom's boyfriend broke into the home on Christmas, beat her up, and robbed the house while Tony hid in the closet.

By the time he and his peers were grappling with the onset of puberty, Tony was experiencing what he can see looking back was deep depression. At the time, he didn't have the language or the emotional literacy to name what was going on with him; he was mainly focused on just getting through the day. But thoughts like *I won't live long* and *The world will be better without me* would pass through his mind as he walked through the halls to racist jeers about his appearance, as he experienced bullying, and as he was left out of after-school activities.

Eventually, his mom arranged for him to switch schools. But this was a Band-Aid solution. The bullies may have been the immediate problem, but the underlying issue was Tony's Body Grief, resulting from his untreated depression—depression that had deep roots in the injustice of what it means to be a Black man in America.

As it turned out, changing schools only dialed up the volume on Tony's emotional turmoil. Everything was supposed to be "fine" now, but it was here that he made an attempt to take his own life. Thankfully, he survived, although he went on to experience substance abuse as a way of self-medicating his mental health issues. After all, Tony had also learned that to be a man he must avoid or hide his emotions, and not show any sign of weakness to others.

Through community, Tony did eventually find healing for his addictions. He also got married and had a child of his own, a daughter.

But it wasn't until his midthirties when he was finally able to name his Body Grief and begin his real healing. As he describes, "I had gotten to a point where I was actively trying to help myself, and still I wasn't receiving what I needed." When he reached out to family, he was met with claims that he was "crazy" and "bipolar." (Can you see the ableism at play here?) This repeated dismissal led Tony even further into the bad cycle of coping behaviors that he was trying to climb out of. It was his wife who finally sat him down and said, "No more. Something needs to be done."

At this point, they met with a marriage therapist, who was also a Black man. Finally, Tony felt safe to be himself. He asked him, "See me, help me." The therapist agreed.

As Tony opened up, the therapist helped him connect the dots between the trauma of his early life, the racism that had underscored his experiences, and what he had internalized about what it meant to be a man to his current self-destructive behaviors. In these honest, clear-eyed exchanges, Tony was finally able to name his Body Grief. In addition to the feeling the turmoil that his mental health issues and his suicide attempt had created in his body, he had to acknowledge his grief about being in a Black body in a brutally racist society.

Now that he was no longer in denial, and no longer perceived his "defective" body as being the problem, Tony felt his power returning to him. He realized that he needed to be sober, quit his job, and get serious about processing his compounded Body Grief. At age thirty-seven, Tony has even turned his problems into his purpose by creating a mental health group for Black men. His chief motivation? "If I'm not looking after myself and my mental health, what kind of disruption will I create with my wife and daughter?" he asks himself. By naming his Body Grief, Tony is doing what he can to end the cycle of trauma and pay his own healing forward.

Leaning into Body Kindness

As we've learned, in a resolutely unfair and unequal world, it can be so much easier to blame our own bodies for any pain, frustration, and prejudice we may be experiencing than to attempt to confront and disrupt the status quo. But blaming ourselves only perpetuates the unrealistic standards of our ableist society. Not only is treating our bodies with kindness key to working with our Body Grief, in an unjust world it is a revolutionary act.

Body Kindness is what helps us dismantle the myth of a pain-free world and move beyond Perceived Body Betrayal. It looks like tapping into your self-compassion and treating yourself with the tenderness and consideration that you show others when they are experiencing any kind of pain—which, of course, is harder than it sounds. Kindness and self-compassion are often the last things we feel toward our bodies when we perceive them as having failed us. For this reason, practicing Body Kindness is its own act of resistance, pulling us out of Perceived Body Betrayal and back toward Body Trust.

There are many ways to practice Body Kindness. You can:

- Have a warm breakfast within an hour of waking.

- Take a lunch break outside.

- Stretch while taking some deep breaths.

- Take a ten-minute seated yoga break at your work desk.

- Sleep in for an extra half hour.

- Say no to any plans that you feel stressed about.

- Say yes to any plans you feel excited about.

- Take a bath with scented Epsom salts.

- Ask for a hug.

- Rest with a warm compress for any body parts that hurt.

The kinder we are to our bodies, the more opportunities we give them to rest, heal, and simply be. And the more we do that, the more in tune we become with our bodies and their changes. This is what Casey discovered when she received a blood cancer diagnosis in her late twenties.

As Casey describes it, her body was "speaking" to her for about a year before she got her diagnosis. First it spoke in whispers, and then it started to get *loud*. Initially, Casey dismissed the red flags her body was waving in her face, but she quickly realized that something was seriously wrong. Her own prior experience with eating disorder recovery had taught her how to properly listen to her body and honor her bodily cues. Now she began to listen intently.

It started with a nagging cough and relentless fatigue. Time and again, her doctor told her nothing was up—but her body kept telling her something was wrong. The cough would not let up, which made her return to her doctor again and again, until finally a scan came back abnormal, and she got her cancer diagnosis. After so long trying to find an answer, things started moving quickly and Casey had no time to process her emotions. "All I felt was anger at being dismissed for so long," she shared when we spoke.

As she began treatment, her life changed overnight, the Body Grief blooming like the cancer in her body. Within a month of being diagnosed, Casey experienced rapid weight gain from the steroids and chemotherapy she was prescribed. She developed "moon face," lost all of her hair, and couldn't partake in any of the activities she used to enjoy. On top of everything, she also couldn't be intimate with her husband, or even share a bathroom with him because of the risk it posed to her weak immune system. This triggered wave after wave of Body Grief. Casey felt defeated.

It would have been so easy for Casey to perceive her body as being broken or having failed her. But her years of body image work helped her stay out of Perceived Body Betrayal, until eventually she was able to feel deep gratitude for her body's ability to take in a literal poison in order to save her life.

"No matter what this means for the look and functionality of my body, I am thankful," she told me.

Casey endured eight grueling months of cancer treatment. Even on days when she thought she wouldn't make it from one side of the bed to the other, her ability to use Body Kindness to stay in Body Trust helped her to keep going. Casey was able to see her body as her partner throughout her treatment; her body was her ally. On hard days, Casey speaks out loud to her body, encouraging it with loving words:

> I know how hard you are working to regenerate my nerves and my brain and my tissue. I understand that this means you will signal pain to me and cause me to forget things and not be able to form sentences or have difficulty breathing. It makes sense! You've been through SO much. I'm so proud of you! You got this. One breath at a time. One step at a time. One nerve at a time. We are in this together. Thank you for fighting for me. I may need to have a few cries today, and I may get frustrated at how different you feel. Just know that I still love you.

Body Grief is a beautiful mess of a journey. It is cyclical, nonlinear, and it can be incredibly lonely and painful. But Casey can reflect today on how her year of cancer and chemo led to an even deeper sense of Body Trust—the opposite of Perceived Body Betrayal. Yes, what she experienced was unfair. It hurts, and naming and staying connected to her Body Grief means continually acknowledging how different her body is from day to day, and how foreign it feels at times. This sucks, and it is painful, and frustrating as hell. But staying with her Body Grief also helps Casey practice gratitude and compassion for the body she is in.

AFFIRMATIONS

"My body is on my side."

"It is safe to be in my body today."

"We are here again and that is okay."

JOURNAL PROMPTS

My Body Grief is . . .

My body speaks to me by . . .

In the eyes of society my body is . . .

THREE

Dismissal:
I Am Not Okay

After going through puberty at age fifteen, Sydney suddenly started experiencing debilitating daily headaches, vomiting, vertigo, and visual disturbances. A nationally ranked competitive tennis player, dancer, and musical theater kid, she desperately wanted to feel like a "normal" teenager again, so she went to extreme lengths to avoid the truth of what she was experiencing. In her unwillingness to confront her Body Grief, she would frequently lie in the fetal position in her parents' closet when her symptoms became overwhelming, and take Advil daily to mask her symptoms, all while convincing herself that all she needed to feel better was a nap.

Over time, Sydney's condition grew progressively worse. She was, in fact, experiencing severe craniocervical and atlantoaxial instability due to her yet undiagnosed genetic illness: like me, she had Ehlers-Danlos syndrome. But she'd become so good at masking the severity of her symptoms that when she finally did go to a doctor, she was not listened to, taken seriously, or even properly tested. Instead, she was sent home with a diagnosis of anxiety and an eating disorder—all of which were secondary to her underlying medical issues.

Secretly, Sydney knew the diagnoses she'd received didn't add up. Her migraines didn't explain her inability to walk, and the eating disorder diagnosis didn't fully account for what was actually an inability to keep food down. Besides, she wasn't experiencing any body image distortions and yearned to be able to eat normally. But Sydney felt she had no right to argue with her doctors. She went home with even more doubts.

Dismissal:
The First Phase of Body Grief

Dismissal is the first stage of Body Grief, though it can come and go in waves throughout the entire cycle. We enter Dismissal when we, like Sydney, try to stay in control of the narrative about what's happening to and in our bodies that we can't make sense of. Instead of acknowledging what's going on, we say, "I'm fine, everything's fine." After all, no one wants to be the problem child, especially if you already have a track record of being just that (all my middle children, raise your hands!).

Ultimately, Dismissal is a response to fear: fear of what is happening to us. Fear of inconveniencing ourselves and others with an uncomfortable truth. Fear about what the future holds. Fear that we will never go back to how we were before. When we are in Dismissal, a little voice in the back of our head tells us, "Once I say it out loud, I will have to face whatever this is." The truth—that we are far from fine, that our body is changing and that we are in Body Grief—is too inconvenient, too troubling, too confusing, or too painful to be with right now.

But left unacknowledged, Dismissal becomes a deep form of self-betrayal, as it prevents us from tapping into our mind-body-spirit connection and keeps us out of alignment with our body and its needs. I call this alignment Body Attunement, and it is integral to strengthening our capacity for Body Trust. But when things are changing fast, our body stops "performing," or we are in pain, it can be so scary to confront what is really happening in our body that we can slip into Dismissal without even being aware this is occurring. This is the nature of the beast: we don't *want* to acknowledge what's happening, so Dismissal swoops in as we deny whatever is causing us to experience Body Grief in the first place.

SIGNS YOU ARE IN DISMISSAL

How can you tell you are in Dismissal? You may find yourself wishing things would go back to "normal" and acting as if everything is fine when it's clearly not. Thoughts about being seen as too much, too needy, or too difficult may crowd in, even as you do your best to ignore the very real symptoms that you are experiencing—even if these include pain, anxiety or depression, skin and weight changes, difficulty breathing, and other kinds of physical discomfort. You might downplay what you are experiencing, gaslighting yourself to beat others to the punch: "I'm in so much pain during my periods . . . but probably not as much as other women." "I no longer feel I have control over my body as a new mother . . . but that's the price we pay!"

Dismissal can also often show up in isolation and withdrawal. You might find it easier to cancel plans with friends and ignore text messages for fear that someone may notice what is going on. Or perhaps you start overworking, packing your calendar with meetings, work functions, and deadlines to further prove to yourself and the world that you are indeed "fine," and to distract yourself from what is happening in your body. You might also find yourself doomscrolling while partially tuning into the streaming service in the background as you binge on information to dissociate. Anything to keep you in your head and out of the chaos of your body can be a sign of Dismissal.

But the longer we are unable to acknowledge our Dismissal, the more likely it can morph into depression. Over time, it can get harder to connect to the things that once brought you joy. Ultimately, you might develop maladaptive coping mechanisms like self-harming and eating disorders. Although a lot of people may think this is a way of seeking attention, this kind of coping is actually meant to *divert* attention from what is really happening, so we don't have to deal with whatever underlying issues are the root cause of our Body Grief.

External Dismissal: "There Is Nothing Wrong with You"

Oftentimes, what makes this phase even more sticky is that our own Dismissal of what we are experiencing is compounded by what I call External Dismissal, or the dismissal others project onto us. While fear and avoidance may be what drive us into Dismissal, it tends to be the people around us who keep us there. In Sydney's case, it was her doctor, and in Tony's case, we saw his suffering prolonged by the systemic silencing and invalidation of Black people's pain.

Can you relate to either of these examples? Perhaps you have confided in a friend or family member that you think something is wrong, only for them to "reassure" you that it's probably all in your head.

After all, they don't want you to be hurting, either. Plus, if your own Dismissal has already told you that what you're experiencing is not that big of a deal, why would anyone want to disagree?

Unfortunately, even if our body is telling us something different, having our own Dismissal validated by External Dismissal can keep us stuck in this phase indefinitely. After all, when things feel out of control in our body, we *want* to believe doctors. They know better than us, don't they? The surface-level comfort of being told "You're fine, my love" by a well-meaning friend or relative can also be very seductive, and when it comes to the systemic dismissal of our pain, often we have no option but to keep powering through. But all of this can be a huge roadblock to us getting the help we need.

In the beginning stages of my chronic illness journey, my internal Dismissal of the seriousness of my condition was validated by External Dismissal from the medical professionals from whom I sought help. Even as I began to experience debilitating head and neck pain—to the extent that I was unable to complete basic tasks and began to risk losing my independence—the ER doctors would tell me everything looked normal. But the thing is, normal is only "normal" when you are tested *against* what would be a cause for concern; what looks normal, therefore, is entirely subjective. Given that I was already struggling to get through the day, I didn't have the energy to fight back, let alone advocate for additional tests. But on a deeper level, I also wanted to believe the doctors—to believe that *I was fine*. It felt easier and less scary than acknowledging what was really happening in my body.

But the Dismissal spell broke when I found myself in the ER for the eighth time, and my mom called and demanded to be put on speakerphone to talk to the doctor.

"Jayne has been in and out of the ER for weeks now," she said. "She has a habit of downplaying her symptoms, and because she is young and 'looks good' doctors dismiss her all the time. I am a nurse,

I know something is wrong here, and I will not let my daughter leave the hospital tonight. I am worried about meningitis. Do your due diligence!"

The doctor replied, "I mean, I'm always excited to do procedures, and I'd be happy to do a spinal tap [lumbar puncture] to test for meningitis. But I don't think your daughter has that, ma'am. I think she just injured her neck."

I felt myself cringe. Why did my mom have to make a fuss? But I was also angry: Who the fuck did this doctor think he was? I hadn't injured my neck. He didn't know anything about me! Meanwhile, the pressure in my head was so intense, it felt like my eyes were being pushed out of my skull from the inside, like a gruesome scene from *Game of Thrones*. I was achy like I had the flu, and all I wanted was for it all to just stop. I felt like I was dying.

In hindsight, I wasn't far off.

Before I knew it, the doctor had snapped on a pair of rubber gloves, assembled his set of shiny, cold, pokey-looking tools, and was asking me to bend over so he could sterilize the area on my back where the needle would be inserted. I was shocked that we were going to do a spinal tap right here in our ER room. As I looked around, I saw a ball of human hair rolling on the ground like a tumbleweed. My gut clenched; this all felt too casual. Wasn't a spinal tap kind of a big deal? But what did I know? I was the patient, and he was the expert, so I didn't say anything.

The doctor was acting so blasé about it all, but it turns out he forgot one very important part: to measure the opening pressure of my spinal cord where my cerebral spinal fluid (CSF) was released. This measurement would have shown an increase in CSF, a small but significant detail that would prove incredibly important later on.

When he finished, the doctor said, "All right, I've patched you up. I'll get that tested for you. Just wait here."

Miraculously, as my husband, Sean, and I waited for the results, I started to feel better. The color came back to my face. I could form sentences, and I was even laughing at Sean's jokes. And when the doctor returned, there it was again: External Dismissal. In a smug tone, he said, "Your tests came back normal."

I was utterly confused, feeling both disappointed and relieved. I just couldn't shake how quickly he was dismissing my pain—and yet how excited he'd been to "experiment" on me. But I was feeling better, so maybe it *had* all been in my head. I was sent home with some Valium, eager to get back to life as "normal." And there it was again: my own Dismissal of my body's wise intuition.

The next day, I saw clients and resumed my usual workout routine. I even went swimming in the pool that weekend (nobody told me you're supposed to wait six to eight weeks before swimming after a spinal tap). "See, I'm fine!" I told myself. But five days later I couldn't see. Walking was a struggle as my balance was off-kilter, and my pain was at an eight out of ten. By the time I ended up in the ER again, I felt like I was going crazy.

But this time my mom was in town, and she was loud enough and advocated hard enough for me that the hospital brought in the neurosurgery team. I was immediately admitted to the hospital, where I was told that I most likely had a brain tumor, sent up for an MRI, and given another spinal tap, this time checking the opening pressure. The results showed that I did not have a brain tumor and was in fact experiencing pseudotumor cerebri, also known as intracranial hypertension. The excess CSF this creates causes pain, loss of sight, nausea, vomiting, loss of balance, and ringing in the ears, among other symptoms I was experiencing. The reason I felt better after the initial spinal tap was that the excess fluid being drained had relieved the pressure on my brain.

When I finally received my diagnosis, I felt both stunned and validated. All of my symptoms and pain had been real all along, but my own internal Dismissal had been validated by the doctors' External Dismissal. Like so many of us, I had been silenced, and therefore I continued to silence myself. I had downplayed what was going on each step of the way because *I didn't want to believe what was happening.* I'd been recovered from my eating disorder for years; I just wanted to live my life already! So I ignored my intuition, second-guessed myself, and dismissed the cues my body was giving me, which in turn led me to accept my doctors' skepticism as I experienced debilitating pain and even loss of vision. The old internalized ableist belief that I was too much, that I wasn't deserving of the time and attention it would take to get to the bottom of what I was experiencing, had reared its head again.

Exercise:

AM I (DIS)MISSING SOMETHING?

If you are having a tough time deciding if you need support for what is going on in your body right now, creating a cost-benefit analysis of your current state, both physical and emotional, can help bring clarity in the face of Dismissal. Costs are the symptoms, uncomfortable feelings, and challenges of your current condition that are costing you time, money, patience, livelihood. Benefits are everything that is working for you in your current condition. Make a list of each.

Once you complete the costs and benefits list, ask yourself: Is this functional? Is this the life you want to be living right now? Settling for "fine" is not good enough! Assess the results as if you are reviewing a good friend's. This can sometimes give us more self-compassion. If the costs outweigh the benefits, that's okay. It's time to lean into the reality that things are hard, that this is not your fault, and that you can advocate for yourself and get support to hold you in your Body Grief.

Here's an example of a cost-benefit analysis from a new mom who just gave birth and is experiencing Dismissal around her lack of body autonomy, being "touched out," having difficulty with breastfeeding, and experiencing mood swings. Her narrative sounds like "I should be fine right now; this is what other new moms go through. I have no right to complain. If they can do it, so can I."

COSTS:

- Very little and poor sleep
- Lack of appetite
- Little to no time to eat and nourish myself
- Lonely and isolated
- Tied to a breastfeeding schedule
- Anxiety and fear that the baby is not getting enough nourishment
- Doubt that I am doing a good enough job
- Bleeding and chafed nipples
- Physical pain
- Little time for self and personal hygiene
- Feeling hopeless

BENEFITS:

- Bonding with baby
- Benefits of breastfeeding for baby's long-term health
- Positive feedback from family + friends

We Live in a World That Dismisses Our Needs

Unfortunately, we live in an ableist society that rewards hyper-independence and perfectionism above asking for help and having needs. This is a very Westernized point of view; many other cultures foster and value community over independence. But when our worth is predicated on our ability to perform, the idea of needing and accepting help from your community can feel inherently *wrong*. If you can't take care of yourself, you have too many needs. If you reach out for help, you must be weak. If you are weak, you are worthless. Ugh. Can you see how this kind of thinking rewards Dismissal when Body Grief arises?

The idea of some bodies not being "worthy" is ableist in itself: Who gets to decide what is worthy and what isn't? It is human to be vulnerable and to have needs, and it is humane to ask for and receive help. To help us get better at spotting when we are in Dismissal, let's take a deeper look at why dismissing our needs has become such a cultural go-to, especially as it pertains to our Body Grief.

I recently had a conversation with a dear friend of mine, who is a fellow therapist. We always laugh about our lives and trauma when we are together, because, well, you have to! This time, we shared a joint, and she opened up to me about the raw truths of balancing life as an entrepreneur with her roles as a wife and a mother of three teen-age children, along with her stress around managing her health and just trying to be a human and have some fun. Of course she was frustrated about not being able to get it all done.

Quite high at some point, we stared at a single cupcake sitting on what seemed to be a gigantic cake stand in the center of my kitchen table. My friend stopped midsentence. "So what's with the lonely cupcake?"

We lost it. As our bellies jiggled and our eyes watered with laughter, feeling safe to feel all of our feelings in that moment, she said, "Thanks for letting me be needy." I looked at her and said, "You mean just being a person who has needs?" We started howling again because that is basically what she was apologizing for—having basic human needs. How *dare* she, or any of us, be needy?

It is very inconvenient to be sick or out of action in a culture that runs on and rewards uber-productivity (as in, who can *afford* to be sick?), so it's easier to pretend that everything is fine and just power on through. In my clinical practice, perfectionism and people-pleasing are common traits among the kind of high achievers who often develop eating disorders. And well, perfectionism and people-pleasing are hugely beneficial to a capitalist society that tells us to work hard, and to be small, quiet, and obedient.

Reflection

How has Dismissal manifested for you over the years, and in what ways can you learn from those moments? Were some moments of Dismissal more maladaptive than others? Perhaps you boldly opened up to a doctor about your symptoms, and seeing as your initial lab results came back normal you've kept quiet about your symptoms since, even though they are worsening. Or perhaps you simply noticed some irregular pain while you were working out, but since you felt fine a few minutes later, you just keep on going. How does it feel in your body to revisit these moments? Remember, Dismissal is a normal part of the Body Grief process, and we can always learn from our own maladaptive behaviors.

The Hall Pass That Keeps Us in Dismissal

One way social and cultural forces keep us in Dismissal is the mighty enabler the Hall Pass, what I call any verbal permission slip that allows us to keep engaging with problematic behaviors that are actually symptomatic of the issue and a cause of great distress. A Hall Pass sounds like:

- "You look great!" (when you are in the throes of disordered eating)
- "But you've always been so healthy!"
- "I wish I had your willpower!"
- "Hmmm. Are you drinking enough water?"

It can be issued by a parent, teacher, friend, doctor, or other medical professional, when you express a need for help and instead of intervening, they dismiss you with proof that you are "fine."

Being issued a Hall Pass can sometimes feel as if you are getting away with something. Deep down you want somebody to validate your Body Grief. But because naming our Body Grief can be a scary big step, you take the Hall Pass and run with it. This is something I see all the time in my client work, as Hall Passes are regularly issued to people with eating disorders—especially if their symptoms do not manifest in ways that are commonly portrayed in the media, like sunken cheeks, a skeletal body, and hair falling out. The reality is, it is hard to identify if somebody has an eating disorder just by looking at them. People with EDs can exist in bigger bodies, they may be incredibly "health-conscious" and "fit," or their weight may never visibly fluctuate.

Due to the prevalence of fatphobia, even if thinness *is* the result of the disease, it is often seen as desirable, so someone with an ED may be praised for the very thing that is causing them pain. In addition, lack of understanding in the medical profession surrounding these disorders (i.e., the assumption that this is a "white women's disease") means eating disorders are consistently dismissed in people of color and people who don't identify as women or may not present as feminine.

Hall Passes are also frequently granted to those with conditions you can't necessarily see, such as chronic illness and mental illness. A "You look good," a "You seem fine," or a "You are so strong and resilient" all sound harmless enough—but each carries a powerful undercurrent of dismissal to those with invisible illnesses.

My client Louise experienced multiple Hall Passes over the course of her sixteen-year struggle with her eating disorder. Having been put on a diet at age eight by her parents, she was praised for not eating, for her weight loss, for counting calories, and for overexercising. Her anorexia started with cutting the crust off a sandwich and asking for the low-fat Skippy peanut butter, because that's the kind that

"Grandma ate." It manifested in eating carrots and cucumbers and drinking water when what she was really hungry for was a robust snack. It had her measuring cereal in the morning and packing her own lunch so that she knew what was going into her body at all times, all at the tender age of ten.

Louise received a direct Hall Pass from her friends' parents, who praised her for being "the healthiest kid they had yet to meet." Her eating habits were "smart and independent" in the eyes of adults. In middle school, she started Weight Watchers with her mom under the guise of "self-confidence" and "getting spring-break-ready," which in turn created a codependent relationship with numbers. Calories, weight, BMI, inches, clothing size: it all started to dictate her value, and any time the numbers went up, she doubled down on her restrictive eating. But she was keeping up in school, exceeding in some classes even. Every time Louise was praised for the eating disorder behaviors and appearance, it gave her a Hall Pass that pulled Louise even deeper into her eating disorder and her Body Grief.

As for the parents of close friends who started to notice Louise's odd behaviors around food, the teachers who asked about her high anxiety and lack of concentration in class, and the friends who commented on her rapid weight loss, they were dismissed by my client and her parents as being "silly" or "nosy," or told that they didn't know what they were talking about. All because they were not ready to face the truth, and because the whole family had received enough Hall Passes along the way to help them dismiss Louise's suffering.

Meanwhile, Louise was suffering in silence. No matter how little food she consumed, or how much she tried to manipulate her biology, she couldn't stand the feeling of being in her body; this alone triggered so much Body Grief. But everyone said she was fine, so she shouldn't worry either, right?

By the time Louise reached out to me, she was in her late twenties, had been in and out of numerous treatment centers, and had accumulated significant medical trauma due to the amount of External Dismissal she had experienced. She was mired in her own Dismissal as well: although she was what was considered weight restored, in her eyes this meant she was "too large for my liking."

"I really am fine," she would tell me. "I've never been this heavy, I don't understand why I still need all this help."

In our work together, I helped Louise see that Dismissal had crept in because for a long time, she feared that she would not get the help she needed because she didn't look sick enough. Every time her parents, friends, and doctors had granted her a Hall Pass from confronting the underlying causes of both her eating disorder and her resulting Body Grief, she had been dismissed. This in turn only confirmed the convenient belief that she was, indeed, fine, and that she did not need or deserve help.

My work was to guide Louise to trust that showing up for herself was paramount, and that choosing recovery and kindness was key, even if she didn't believe it would work. So much of the work we did together was met with ambivalence—a defense mechanism to every Hall Pass she had been given over the years, and to all the internal and External Dismissal within her very real Body Grief. But the truth was, she still needed help, because she still deserved so much more out of life. Once she accepted this, Louise was finally able to start to live a life beyond restriction.

No matter the decades of Dismissal that have accumulated, or the number of Hall Passes you have received, it is never too late to advocate for yourself and get help. Sometimes resistance shows up when we need healing the most, and Louise's story is a beautiful depiction of this. Following years of Hall Passes and medical trauma, her fight finally came to a head when we started working together, as she was finally given permission to acknowledge her Body Grief and phase out of her Dismissal. Sometimes it is when we are at the point of most resistance within our internal Dismissal that we are closest to moving into one of the other six phases.

Reflection

Take a moment to reflect on what has been coming up for you while reading. In your experience of living in your body, what social and cultural factors have taught you to down-play your needs? Have you ever been granted a Hall Pass to stay in Dismissal? Reflecting on this may bring up one or more of what I call "ricochet" moments: times when you have dipped your toes into the Ocean of Body Awareness, only to realize that you are unlikely to get the help you truly need—and so you pull your toe right back out. That moment right there, the retraction of the toe, is Dismissal.

Perhaps I Am Not Okay: Moving through Dismissal

When we are plunged into Body Grief, oftentimes our first instinct is to use denial and Dismissal to distance ourselves from what is hap-pening in our body. In the process, we become disconnected from our physical reality—even as our body does its best to signal to us what is going on. The first step to working through Dismissal is to restore a deep sense of connection with your body, then you can begin to ad-vocate for yourself.

PRACTICE BODY RESIDENCY

One way to connect to our bodies is to practice Body Residency: acknowledge that your body is your forever home, whether you are content in it or not. No matter how much you alter your body, in the end, it is your vessel, and when we practice Body Residency we claim it as such. After all, no matter what is going on inside, *your body is where you live your life*. Staying in Dismissal is like sleeping on the street outside your own front door.

When I was little, my mom would wake me up, make me a bowl of cereal, and then have me lie on the floor and do the "clock stretch," which is where you basically move your body like the arms of a clock, while Loonette the Clown and her doll Molly played in the background. Little did I know I was practicing Body Residency every single day at that young age. To do this yourself, every morning, right when your alarm goes off, take a deep breath and stretch. With each stretch, bring your awareness to how your muscles feel, how the breath moves through your body, and how your heart is beating. Remind yourself: *You belong in this body, your body belongs with you. This is your home, and no one can take that away from you.*

Of course, there are many ways to practice Body Residency. The key is to maintain awareness of how your body feels. Other ways to safely and securely "be" in your body include meditation, intuitive eating, breathwork, and doing a body scan, a mindful walk, tai chi, a self-massage, or some chair yoga.

Because Body Residency helps build Body Trust, the more you can start to implement this practice into your life, the less time you will spend in Dismissal. Over time, this becomes a two-way street: the less you dismiss your body, the more welcoming a home it will become. The roof may still have a leak and there may still be a lot of dusty old furniture up in the attic, but now you now have a cozy fire and a well-stocked pantry. Your home is stocked with the supplies you need to get through the hard times.

As you practice Body Residency, you will likely notice that you are less keen to change the subject or revert to "I'm fine" the next time somebody asks you how you are doing. That you feel more confident answering honestly, and that you have more capacity to hold any emotions that arise as you acknowledge *this is Body Grief.* From a more embodied place, rather than a place of judging your own feelings, you will become better skilled at simply observing what is coming up. You will begin to see that claiming your Body Residency means claiming your truth.

ACTIVATE YOUR INNER ADVOCATE

Once you have reestablished residency in our body, you'll be better placed to activate a powerful helper who can help you move past Dismissal: your Inner Advocate. In an ideal world, we would all have a fierce supporter like my mom by our side to help us get what we need when we are in Dismissal. Hearing her voice on the phone in the ER was exactly what I needed to feel like I could stand up for myself, leading to my first life-saving diagnosis. But we don't always have an actual person fighting in our corner. In those moments, we can call on our Inner Advocate to help us speak up on our own behalf.

Your Inner Advocate might let its presence be known in the tightness in your gut when your doctor tells you, "Everything looks great!"—but you came all this way because you don't *feel* great. Or it might be a little voice in your head urging you to open up more to your spouse at the dinner table after they insist, "But you seem fine to me!" when you've expressed a worry. Perhaps it shows up as constant ruminating on something that just "doesn't feel right," or a tickle in the back of your throat, like you are about to vomit as the stress hormones cause you to sweat through your blouse.

At first, it can take a few tries to activate your Inner Advocate. This is what I experienced at my eight-week post-op appointment from the total hysterectomy that followed my endometriosis diagnosis. With two external uterine fibroids, stage two endometriosis, I was experiencing severe hemorrhaging for two weeks out of every month. One solution would have been to get an IUD fitted, but this was not available to me due to my neurological disorder and my body rejecting the hardware that had been previously placed in my body. Therefore, several specialists had finally recommended a hysterectomy. The surgeon looked at his computer and said, "Yep, we found a polyp and some cancerous and precancerous cells in the uterus." He said it like he was ordering lunch, so flat, so blasé, that I had to take a moment.

"Isn't that abnormal for someone under the age of thirty-five?" I asked.

"Yes," he replied, "I can't explain it." He clicked out of his notes and looked at me. I didn't want to say anything else, because the more I asked, the more answers I would get that I wasn't ready to hear. I wanted to stay in control, but I was mainly tired of feeling like an inconvenience, of asking questions that dug deeper than the doctors wanted to dig. *Then again*, I thought, *every time I've empowered my Inner Advocate to speak up, I've been right.*

While I didn't speak up in that appointment, a few weeks later, my Inner Advocate had me find a new doctor and get a second opinion. That doctor took my concerns seriously and advised that I get on a waiting list to see an oncologist, just to be safe.

To access your own Inner Advocate when you are experiencing internal or External Dismissal, the first step is to take a deep breath and say out loud, "I am not fine." It can be challenging to be honest and not run from your body's truth, given how hard, scary, foreign, or uncharted the waters ahead might be. Some helpful language for this might be:

- "Something isn't right, and I believe my body. What other options do we have?"

- "I am not leaving until I have answers."

- "I know my body, and I have taken the steps to come here. It is your job to do the rest."

- "I am ready to learn with you."

- "I will not allow you to give up on me; my body has fought too hard."

- "I trust in myself, and I will not allow you to dismiss my truth."

It could even be helpful to visualize your Inner Advocate as a character who lives in your head and you can call on when you need them. Perhaps even give them a spandex superhero outfit—or imagine them as that badass character with all the witty comebacks from your favorite movie. Practice with whatever works for you, and with awareness, patience, and trust, this voice will learn to respond fiercely in the face of any internal and External Dismissal.

Until you have gotten used to using it, your Inner Advocate could be full of nerves—so be kind to yourself as it learns to speak up. And if you can't hear its whispers yet, remember that this Inner Advocate is in all of us. It is there in our pain, our fear, and our discomfort—and it is there in our Body Grief.

Ultimately, Dismissal is a deeply engrained psychological and cultural response to the pain and inconvenience of our Body Grief. Thanks to both our internal fears and the external systems of oppression that make little space for our human needs, staying stuck here can find us living in a sort of twilight zone, where everything is murky and we constantly second-guess our reality. This in turn keeps us from feeling and healing our Body Grief. Practicing Body Residency helps us move past Dismissal. Finding our fierce Inner Advocate empowers us to speak up when we have been silenced—either by our own fears or by External Dismissal from others. And somewhere in this process of moving through our Dismissal, we will come up against the second phase of Body Grief: Shock.

AFFIRMATIONS

"My intuition can be trusted."

"My experience is real and valid."

"I know my body and my body is wise."

JOURNAL PROMPTS

I dismiss my Body Grief when I . . .

When I am dismissed by others it feels like . . .

My Inner Advocate sounds like . . .

FOUR

Shock: This Is
Really Happening

~~

A hysterectomy may be the best option at this point."

My reaction when the doctor told me that the only solution to my endometriosis was to remove my uterus was relief; I would finally be done with my pain and discomfort. At the time, I instantly blocked out what this would mean for me beyond that, because behind his words lay yet another impossible truth: I would be infertile at age thirty-one.

I received the news about the hysterectomy on a long-awaited consult at the Mayo Clinic, where I expected to finally receive some answers and a treatment plan for my gynecological health. The full impact of this development would not hit until seven months later, and nearly four months after the operation itself. My three laparoscopic scars still swollen and red, I came across an endearing video while scrolling on social media of a young mother taking her eager six-year-old daughter to her first Taylor Swift concert—an artist who played constantly in the background as I wrote this book. It was adorable. My heart was so happy watching the young girl burst into tears when Taylor came onstage at the Eras Tour. The crowd of seventy thousand fans went wild, unleashing three years of pandemic isolation and heartbreak as they screamed "Cruel Summer" in unison, and my inner child rejoiced along with them.

I can't wait to do that with my daughter one day.

The thought popped casually into my head. And then—*bam*—reality hit me like a lightning bolt. *You won't get to do that, Jayne. You will never be a mother. You no longer have a home for a baby to grow.*

A moment of pure Shock plunged me into the depths of my Body Grief.

Shock: When Reality Bites

The second stage of Body Grief swoops in when there is no more room for Dismissal. It is no longer possible or feasible to ignore the reality of what we are experiencing, and so we are confronted with the truth: there is no more pretending or going back. We will have to live with our body exactly as it is. In this way, Shock is the embodiment of a reality check.

Shock can pass in seconds or last for days, but something usually triggers it. You might receive a diagnosis, break a limb, start to lose your hair, no longer fit into your favorite pair of jeans, hit a metaphorical rock bottom, or get a reminder of how things used to or can no longer be, like when I saw the video of a mother taking her daughter to the Taylor Swift concert. You realize you are completely out of control, and your brain struggles to come to terms with this. You might think, *I can't do this*, or *I am overwhelmed*, or *This feels intolerable.*

In many ways, the other phases of Body Grief can be easier to process, in that they aren't as emotionally potent. Shock can be violent. It forces self-awareness without our permission and can manifest as a painful and electrifying jolt to the physical and emotional systems as we realize that our body is no longer what it used to be. But it can also leave us feeling numb, like we are floating outside of our physical body, and the resulting overwhelm and disbelief can present as complacence or paralysis. It's natural to want to dissociate from Shock. Becoming present to the Shock of our Body Grief can feel like our world is being turned upside down.

When I talk to clients, friends, and colleagues about this phase of Body Grief, they often tell me they're scared that this is where life as they know it ends. "If I allow myself to go there, I fear I won't come out of it," they say. And in many ways, they're right: there is no off switch for our Body Grief. Shock plunges us into the Ocean of Body Awareness, bringing all the suppressed realities, beliefs, and emotions of our Body Grief to the fore. Even if there is a happy ending to our condition, chances are it is a long way off and there will be untold challenges along the way.

The reality is, our bodies are vulnerable, but they are also built to change and adapt. Sometimes these changes and adaptations are painful, messy, and inconvenient, and they stop us from getting what we believe we desire, or what we believe we need. But this is the human condition. Shock only forces us to accept it.

SIGNS YOU ARE IN SHOCK

Shock is, well, shocking, but it can still be hard to spot when we are in this phase. Entering Shock feels like being blindsided, as if we have been hit with something out of the blue. This may be accompanied by an onset of extreme emotions, and your anxiety may start spiraling as you obsess about the future. You might either feel paralyzed by your current reality, or feel like running from reality. In fact, when we enter the Shock phase of Body Grief, it is common to quickly revert to Dismissal as a way of dissociating from a truth that is too challenging to face head-on in the moment.

Dissociation is similar to Dismissal—both of which are coping mechanisms, the latter being about avoidance, and the former being an attempt to completely deny the reality of what we are experiencing. Being able to recognize that you are dissociating is in itself a key sign that you are in Shock. Dissociation may present in different ways for different people, depending on your personality type and levels of resiliency, but it can manifest in self-harm, an unhealthy relationship with food or exercise, overworking, endlessly scrolling on social media, and other behaviors that allow us to numb our fear and pretend that everything is business as usual. When you're in Shock, your body will naturally look for ways to regulate your nervous system—reaching for a stiff drink is one way to do this, as alcohol is a downer that counteracts adrenaline.

For example, during the pandemic and the racial reckoning of 2020, a lot of us experienced Shock anytime we turned on the news or glanced at our social media feeds and so leaned on substances to help us dissociate. According to the National Library of Medicine, binge drinking increased an estimated 40 percent among women during this period. For those of us taking our meals in isolation, absorbing the Shock of what the world was experiencing, a desire to remain in control also led to higher rates of disordered food and diet habits, including overexercising, orthorexia (an obsession with "clean eating"), and binge eating. In both instances, Body Grief is wrapped up in grief for how the pandemic robbed us of our bodily safety and agency overnight.

Dissociation can also show up in what I call the "fixers," or thoughts and statements such as "It doesn't matter what other people think!" and "Just live your life!" These internal and external fixers don't want to see us upset or in pain, because it is too shocking to accept that life in a body is vulnerable, painful, and unfair. So they rush in to quiet our fears and mask our pain with Pollyanna statements and Band-Aid solutions. But what these knee-jerk reactions really do is shove our fear, anger, and frustration deep down so they are hidden from our psyche. This is also where we see Dismissal and Shock vacillate and blend together, as all the phases of Body Grief naturally do from time to time.

What makes dissociation so attractive is that it works—but this is only true for a short time. When we remain in a dissociative state, rather than feeling and fully processing our feelings of uncertainty, we can't move toward healing. The only way to work with Shock is to find ways to confront and accept our reality *exactly as it is*.

Reflection

Take a moment to reflect on a time when Shock swept in like a tropical storm. Remember to always start with naming your Body Grief and work from there. If your Shock has been triggered by seeing a photo that shows the extent of your hair loss, tell yourself, "This is Body Grief." If Shock has hit while watching a game after sustaining an injury, and you realize you will never play that sport again, say it: "This is Body Grief." The tightening in your chest, the suffocating heartbreak, the fear, the anger, the frustration, the feeling of *why me?* This is Shock, and *this is Body Grief*.

This Is Really Happening: From Shock to Acceptance

Being shocked into facing the truths of our Body Grief can be terrifying—but it is also healing. The key to moving through this phase is to accept your body's new reality. To accept that we can no longer move like we used to, that we can no longer fit into our favorite pair of jeans, that these wrinkles are here to stay, that getting up in the middle of the night to pee will be a regular occurrence, and that you now need medication every morning with your coffee. Only from a place of acceptance are we able to stay connected to our body and its needs, and to keep moving away from Perceived Body Betrayal and back toward Body Trust. When we become an honest observer of our experience without rushing to "do" anything to try to fix it, we can just be. Nobody wants to be reliant on mobility aids, just like nobody wants to be in chronic pain, with a pseudotumor and an immune system that is attacking its own body. I certainly would not wish this on anyone! But this is *my* reality, and just like all of us, my only option if I want to keep actually living is to adjust and adapt.

When we accept reality exactly as it is, we become able to change how we relate to that reality. This is the key purpose of the Shock phase of Body Grief. In some ways, Shock has the flavor of a horror movie reveal: *my biggest fear is here*. But it jolts us out of the haze, pushing us through Dismissal so that we can confront our Body Grief head-on. Only then can we both address the causes of our grief and acknowledge what has been lost, as well as the implications of this loss. In the context of menopause, the loss means you are no longer "fertile" and you are no longer "young." This may find you questioning your worth as a person, as you confront your internalized ageism and your relationship with your values. Who will you be now that your fertility is behind you?

But how do we do this? Identifying what a loss means to us often begins by recognizing the expectations we have been holding on to about how our bodies should look like and operate. Which brings us back to entitlement: most of us believe we are entitled to our mobility, or to a "clean bill of health" due to the influencer-approved lifestyle protocols we have been pursuing. Or perhaps we believe we are entitled to abundant fertility, an easy conception, and no hiccups throughout the pregnancy and delivery. The more entrenched these expectations, the heavier the feelings of loss—and the deeper the Body Grief—when they eventually shatter.

Now let's layer on the stories connected to these expectations: What do they say about our worth as a human being and the life we can expect to live? In an ableist society, mobility and health are what make us "whole," while having a "snag-free" pregnancy means being the perfect woman/person, and eventually the perfect mom. When these beliefs are compromised—when we break a leg, get a cancer diagnosis, or are unable to conceive after months of trying—it can be heartbreaking. But confronting our Shock allows us to do the work of dismantling the social scaffolding of our entitlement—that is, the isms of ableism, fatphobia, ageism, racism, sexism, homophobia, and more.

For example, body mass index (BMI) is upheld as a medical-backed way to measure "healthy" weight, but it is actually an archaic tool created by a cis, white, male astronomer who did not include women and people of color in his study, as it "skewed" the results. When we realize this, we see that a lot of us are being held to a racist and sexist standard when it comes to our weight, which frees us to lean out of Shock when we see a certain number on the scale, and into acceptance and Body Trust. In my case, the waves of Shock that followed my hysterectomy helped me acknowledge the internalized misogyny and ableism that tells me my worth as a woman lies in my ability to bear a child. Only by becoming conscious of this am I in a position to write a *new* story about my value in the world. Only when I can accept that a patriarchal, pronatalist world will always see me as less-than for being a childless woman will I get to decide whether I want to hold this belief myself.

Acknowledgment, and most importantly *acceptance*, of our new reality, is what allows us to shift our perspective going forward and move out of Shock. For as long as we are blind to our reality, the stories perpetuated by society will be free to colonize our subconscious.

As you begin to practice accepting your body's new reality, please remember that whatever feelings and sensations accompany Shock, they cannot harm you. You are so brave for doing this. Sadly, I cannot promise you safety. None of us can control the unknown variables that may impact us as human beings, which means safety is never a given when you are living in a body. But I can show you real, actionable tools to help you stay in Shock long enough to be with and begin to accept your new reality.

Exercise:

REALITY CHECKS

Shock can be a reality check. In this exercise, list out any "reality checks" you may have missed in your life and need to acknowledge and grieve as you process this phase of Body

Grief. Some of these reality checks may be more obvious than others. For example, after my hysterectomy, I had two emergency spinal surgeries, during which I was asked if it was possible I was pregnant. It's a routine question, but it slammed me back into my new reality: I no longer have a uterus, cervix, fallopian tubes, or ovaries. My breath was nearly taken away. I was in Shock.

Here are some examples of reality checks:

1. A new friend asking if you want to grab drinks when you are newly sober from substance use.

2. Being invited to a housewarming party that is only accessible by stairs when you are physically disabled.

3. Your partner ordering late-night pizza when you have been diagnosed with celiac disease.

SHIFT DOWN YOUR PERSPECTIVE

A powerful way to work through Shock and move toward acceptance and Body Trust is to practice what I call a Shift Down Perspective. Simply put, adjust your expectations about what your body is entitled to and able to do. This might sound disempowering, but it is actually the opposite. Let me show you what I mean.

Despite the anxiety I experienced as a kid, Little Jayne was raised to believe that she could have it all. Both her body and the ableist society she grew up in would go on to prove differently, but I don't know if I would go back and pop her bubble. She lived. I mean, she really lived, and she was able to live safely and freely as the result of her privilege. She was able to explore the world with curiosity and decide what she wanted for her life.

Honestly, I wish everyone could have that. Rather than take this experience away from my younger self, I would go back and give her better coping skills for when Body Grief would eventually set in— beginning with how to defuse her value from her body's appearance and abilities. I would tell Little Jayne that no one's value lies in their body, and that productivity and looks are not a measure of worth. That way, when life got hard and her body began to change, instead of her Perceived Body Betrayal manifesting as Shock, she would have been able to adopt a Shift Down Perspective to adjust her expectations of her body and the world she was moving through.

We all have expectations of the life we are entitled to—but these expectations are based on our current reality. For example, as a young girl, my value was very much tied to my identity as a dancer, and so my storyline—past, present, and future—revolved around that perspective. I saw my future happiness as being dependent on how my body moved and performed. My sense of worth, achievement, and joy were all tied to the literal leaps and bounds I performed onstage, and to receiving trophies and rounds of applause for what my body could do.

Except I wasn't entitled to shit, remember? None of us are. Nothing about our lives is a given, and radical, earth-shattering change can swoop in at any moment. When my loss of mobility meant I could no longer dance like I used to, the Shock made me feel like giving up, because dissociating felt like the only option. In this phase of Body Grief, I even wondered if life was worth living—after all, disappearing from the planet would be the ultimate way to dissociate. I was terrified to speak this into words because I feared it may be too heavy for my husband and family to hear.

But as I learned to name my Body Grief, I began choosing to shift down my expectations for my life going forward instead. No, I would not be flouncing around the dance floor at my wedding or jumping into the waves at the end of the night, and that sucked, hard. But I would still be dancing—just with a set of wheels attached to me at all times. On that day, I shimmied and shook from the waist up while watching everyone else embody the joy that once held the keys to my worth, whispering to myself, "This is my truth now." My shoulders dropped what felt like three inches from my ears, my jaw unclenched, and I took the largest exhale of my life. And there I was: somehow, I had reached a place of acceptance.

In an ableist world, adopting a Shift Down Perspective can be very hard on the ego. But in our Body Grief process, whenever we are stunned into Shock, it is often the only option if we want to move forward. To be very clear, the Shift Down Perspective is not about silver linings. Instead, it is about finding a new normal that works for you.

Imagine you are visiting Disney World as an adult, a lifelong dream. You can't wait to experience the magical rides from your childhood with your friends and family. However, you are in a different body now. You're bigger, and the years have taken their toll. Perhaps you have a sore neck, and you realize you won't be able to go on Space Mountain. This feels awful. You were so looking forward to revisiting this treasured childhood memory! As your family lines up for the ride, the Shock hits you: you will never be that carefree kid, jumping from ride to ride, again. The realization is like an icy ping to the chest. But while things are different now, it doesn't mean you can't still have your own Disney experience. You get to be the one who takes pictures of everyone after the ride drenched in sweat while you sit in your warm, dry clothes enjoying a delicious churro. The Peter Pan's Flight, Dumbo, and safari rides are more your speed these days. The old thrills might no longer be accessible to you, but that's okay.

Exercise:

FEELING 1–5 PERCENT BETTER

Here's another tool that can help us adopt a Shift Down Perspective. Rather than focusing on a clear-cut solution to your situation, aim to feel just 1–5 percent better. Not only is this a more realistic goal when we are in Shock, but it's also an antidote to all-or-nothing thinking: *I will either eat the entire box of cookies or no cookies at all*, or *I will flood you with all of my feelings and thoughts*, or *I will avoid telling you my feelings and bottle them up completely.*

Consider tangible ways you can feel 1–5 percent better in your current situation. Here are some examples from my life:

1. Spending time away from my phone and out on my porch with my pets.

2. Ordering or cooking a special treat for myself.

3. Running a warm bath with fragrant Epsom salts.

4. Asking my husband for a hug.

5. Playing my favorite song loudly while I dance in the kitchen.

BREATHE INTO THE SHOCK OF YOUR NEW NORMAL

As you begin to shift down your perspective and work through Shock and toward acceptance and Body Trust, you will sometimes fall back on dissociation as a means of coping with the rush of disorienting feelings that accompany this phase. That's okay! One technique that can help us self-regulate in those moments is breathing. It's deceptively simple and almost instinctual: people often remind us to take a deep breath when we're in a state of panic.

Shock can easily trigger our fight, flight, freeze, or fawn response, which essentially shuts down the frontal lobe (the rational part of the brain) and triggers the amygdala to release adrenaline. Known as the "stress hormone," adrenaline speeds up our heart rate while creating a numbing effect to shield our body from pain, helping us react more quickly in a situation that our body perceives as dangerous. This can be helpful, like when we are quite literally in danger, such as in a car crash or natural disaster. But it can also lead to lashing out (fighting), dissociating (fleeing or freezing), or people-pleasing (fawning) when we are in Shock. Staying *with* our reality in these moments—in order to accept and adapt to it—requires us to regulate this nervous system response. Deep breathing practices, and especially breath retention, are what help us do that, keeping oxygen flow to the brain and calming the amygdala. This is a coping mechanism Gretchen's body knew instinctively to reach for when she found herself in Shock.

"Jesus fucking Christ!"

Pain shot through Gretchen's toe as she wrapped her foot with medical tape. At age fifty-four, my friend was facing yet another surgery on her now dislocated toe. She was also late for a meeting with the contractor to discuss plans for her new home, including how a disability elevator could be incorporated into the design. Having been diagnosed with rheumatoid arthritis (RA) in her thirties and now facing Ehlers-Danlos syndrome herself, Gretchen has lived with a degree of physical pain and discomfort for most of her adult life. As she walked slowly to her car, leaning heavily on her loose and weakening joints, she was confronted with the reality of how fragile her body was, and was met with an overwhelming feeling of doom.

Gretchen and her husband have been through hell and back to get to where they are today. With three children, chicken runs in the backyard, and a thriving mental health business, now they were in a place to design their dream custom home. Arriving at the meeting with the contractor, Gretchen eased herself out of her car with a wince of pain. As the contractor showed her his plans, confirming where the elevator would go, the pain spread from her toe until it filled her whole body with an overwhelming sadness. All Gretchen could see in her mind's eye at that moment was herself growing older and frailer as her twin degenerative illnesses slowly eroded her ability, making it harder and harder for her to move around.

She was shocked to find herself picturing her dream home as a prison. How was this her reality? She had lived with her disability for so long, but having a mobility aid—the elevator—*literally built into her new home* made it all feel so final. Even worse, there was no way she felt comfortable voicing this in the meeting. She had no choice but to revert to Dismissal and nod along, expressing excitement about the construction process.

"Nobody knows how to ask what it's like being disabled," she later told me. "So they don't, which creates this awkwardness. Part of me wanted someone, anyone, to acknowledge that having to use a lift *sucks*. It felt so lonely."

Inside, this turned to anger: *Wow, do people even realize what I am living with and what I am dealing with?!* As the wave of Body Grief rolled through her, Gretchen took a deep breath—her body's natural way of seeking to regulate her central nervous system to help her process her Shock.

Gretchen had learned to use her breath to help her in this way.

Through her years of lived trauma and her professional therapeutic practice, this simple practice is what saved her. The power of pausing and intentionally inhaling through the nose for three to five seconds, feeling her lungs expand and her diaphragm contract, followed by the release of a long, slow exhale through her mouth, made it feel as if her worries were being released from her body, bit by bit. She had even learned that one way to ensure she was getting as much oxygen as possible into her lungs was to hold on to fistfuls of ice to encourage full, complete inhales and exhales.

Now, feeling much more grounded, and as the complex mix of thoughts and emotions swirling in her sorted themselves out like a Rubik's cube, she was finally able to acknowledge the source of her distress: *There will be a time when I hit a really heavy decline, and I am terrified.*

Her Shock wanted her to acknowledge her fear about the future, so Gretchen took another deep breath, picturing it. There would be more pain, more surgeries, and she would come to rely on that chair lift. But her journey had already taught her how resilient she was, her emotional resilience built through learning to be with her trauma, not turn a blind eye to the reality of her situation. Years of therapy had also given her the skills to observe her anxiety mindfully while diffusing her cognitive distortions in that moment, and as the meeting drew to a close, Gretchen was able to grasp on to another thought: *It could be me wearing a beer hat in a wheelchair one day, but as long as I am happy and with my family, that's all that matters.*

And for a moment, she found herself orienting back toward Body Trust.

Breathing Techniques for Self-Regulation

BOX BREATHING
Breathe in for a count of four seconds, hold for four seconds, breathe out for four seconds, and hold for four seconds. Repeat four times. To make this even more powerful, imagine you are drawing the walls of a box with each count of breath.

LET IT ALL GO
Another favorite technique of mine, and one I personally find an immense amount of relief from, is the "Let it All Go" breath. Take one big inhale. When your lungs are completely full, open your mouth and sigh the breath out as loud as you possibly can while flopping your tongue out and letting your arms, hands, and legs go limp. Just let it all go until the last drops of air have been squeezed out of your lungs. Do this as many times as you like until you feel relief.

FEEL ALL YOUR FEELINGS

The adrenaline released by our fight, flight, freeze, or fawn response doesn't just help numb any physical pain we may be experiencing, it helps numb our mental and emotional pain, too—meaning that when we are in Shock, it can be difficult to assess what we really feel. What we feel in our Body Grief can be messy, like anger, resentment, deep sadness, even fear. For our own safety, our body literally tells us to push aside our emotions, bottle them up, and tightly vacuum-seal them away somewhere they won't hurt us or slow us down. But as adaptive as this might be in the face of a literal and immediate threat to our survival, emotions are called *feelings* because they are meant to be *felt*, not pushed away.

Our emotions are a big part of what makes us human, connecting our mind, body, and spirit, and sitting at the crux of Body Awareness and Body Trust. When we push down our emotions, we stifle our sense of who we are in the here and now. We become severed from our core values. We are unable to accept the current reality of our bodies, and therefore keep ourselves stuck in Shock.

No matter how painful or confusing they might be, to move through Shock, it is absolutely necessary to feel all your feelings; that is what they are there for. To start, watch your emotions like the weather, calmly noticing them shifting in force, temperature, and form as they arise, as if they were clouds in the sky. Some emotions are "easier" and more accepted, like joy, confusion, and even sadness, in certain situations. Others, not so much, like anxiety, anger, and apathy. As you engage in this practice, you will start to notice that your emotions are always communicating with you, sending signals from your brain to your body, and from your body to the world.

It's not for me to tell you how an emotion feels in your body, but there are some familiar cues you can look out for. For instance, anxiety is often felt as a tightness in the chest or shoulders, or as butterflies and uneasiness in the stomach. Anger is a secondary emotion, in that it cues us to primary emotions such as shame, hurt, or fear, and is often noticed in behaviors first. As you get to know how your emotions speak to you, the key is to not judge whatever you are feeling, and to accept that all your emotions are part of what make you *you*. Remember: feelings are not facts. They are designed to come and go, and the reason they are called *feel*ings is to encourage us to do just that: *feel* them and move forward.

Thankfully, there is no need to do any of this work alone. Finding a good therapist, a support group, or even an empathetic and non-judgmental friend can create a safety net to help you process your feelings. A therapeutic activity, such as journaling, painting, or taking a walk in nature, can also help your body feel all the feels without you needing to "figure things out." Put on your favorite sad playlist and just let it all flow.

Feeling into Shock

Carve out five to ten minutes of sensory relief—void of phones, outside disturbances, and the needs of others—so that you can focus on the experience of being in your body. Next, read the below prompt, which is designed to guide you into a moment or moments of Shock that you may have missed in your Body Grief process.

At what point in this journey do you recall being snapped back into reality with the Shock of Body Grief?

To begin, close your eyes and ears as you bring this situation and the accompanying feelings to mind. Be very gentle with yourself, and ask: *How does this feel in my body? What physical sensations are tied to the feeling of Shock?* Don't be afraid—whatever comes up for you is okay, and you can tap out at any time by simply opening your eyes. Breathe into whatever sensations arise in your body and tell yourself that it is completely safe to feel it all. Ask yourself, how would you describe these feelings to a young person, to let them know that it is okay to be feeling this way? Whatever comes up for you is normal, just let it all flow.

When you're ready, you can open your eyes and continue to reflect in a journal format, whatever feels right to you.

Learning to Be with Your New Reality

Once you have accepted where you and your body are at, the only option going forward becomes learning to live with your new reality. This can be incredibly challenging, and I want you to promise me you will forgive yourself if you retreat from the Ocean of Body Awareness multiple times per day as you practice this.

To help ease you into the new reality of your body, I want to share a tool that I use in both my personal and my professional practice: Exposure and Repetition. The more we expose ourselves to what our body perceives as a stressful or difficult situation, the easier that situation becomes for us to bear. When we do this repeatedly, our tolerance continues to increase, until eventually it becomes normal, and its power to trigger our amygdala is neutralized. The key to working with Exposure and Repetition is to go slow.

If you are uncomfortable with how your body looks right now, I do not recommend starting by staring at your naked body in the mirror. Instead, ease your nervous system by wiggling your feet in the shower and watching the water run over them and down the drain. Taking it one step further, you might stay in your towel a little longer than usual, then take your time putting lotion on your arms and legs before getting dressed, doing all of this while breathing mindfully. Next, you could try looking in the mirror with your towel wrapped around you. Wrap your arms around your chest, close your eyes, and allow yourself to feel the safety of this self-hug. Do this until one day, you find you are able to stand in front of the mirror without any clothes while you're brushing your teeth. Over time, the practice of Exposure and Repetition helps build new neural pathways in the brain, and create muscle memory in the body and trust in the central nervous system.

Let's look at how this helped William as they grappled with their ongoing gender dysphoria following gender reassignment surgery.

WILLIAM'S STORY

William peeled open their eyes and blinked. The light was so bright in the hospital room, it almost felt as if it was burning their pale skin. They could hear the muffled cries of their mom and best friend, sniffles and whispers with a touch of laughter, as if there was happiness underlying their emotions. William felt a sense of relief: they had finally gotten the life-saving gender-affirming surgery they had needed. As William started to cry happy tears, so did their mom and friend. Five years of intense Body Grief and body dysphoria were finally being healed.

Later, the doctor came by to check on everything and asked William if they wanted to see their new chest without the bandages. William, assigned female at birth, was eighteen years old at the time and had been looking forward to top surgery since they were thirteen. Being a heavy-chested trans person had triggered an intense bout of Body Grief and caused severe gender dysphoria, the medical term for the sense of incongruence between experienced gender and the gender assigned at birth. This moment in the hospital had been years in the making, a literal and symbolic unveiling of the real them. William would now be able to present to the world as the person they knew themselves to be. Now there would be no more Dismissal of their true identity.

As the doctor unwrapped the dressing and binder, William's nostrils flared at the pungent coppery scent of blood and plasma.

"And there you go!" said the doctor. "Once the drains are out, it will heal up nicely." William looked down and saw a flat chest for the first time since they were a child. Their vision unobscured, they could now see their entire body down to their feet. *Holy shit.* There were gauze pads covering their nipples, and their chest was covered in black-and-blue bruises and smeared with orange surgical cleaning solution. There were drains coming out of their armpits, and there it was: their body! William hadn't been able to see their whole body like that for their entire postpubescent life. But this was not what they were expecting. Not once during all their counseling in preparation for the surgery had they been prepared for what to do after.

The joy came and went so quickly, as immediately they were plunged into Shock. *What the actual fuck?!* Their gender dysphoria returned in an instant on a tidal wave of vengeance. Those hips, that belly, those curves . . . they were so feminine still. The Shock of seeing their body as if for the first time hit so hard, William was overcome with Body Grief all over again. They wanted so badly to love their new chest, but now they couldn't stop looking at their "child-bearing hips"—*and ugh, why did people have to call it that?*

As they slipped further into their Body Grief, guilt began to creep in:

I should be happy.

How dare I even have these feelings; I am so lucky.

People would do anything for this surgery, I have no right to complain!

They began to view their very natural feelings of Body Grief as "wrong" and "bad."

William's eighteen-year-old brain was trying to make sense of a very complex grievance, and their Shock sent them right into Dismissal. Rather than asking for further counseling, they went on vacation with a friend one week after the surgery, which included a kayaking trip. They now look back on that excursion and call it what it was: indirect self-harm.

William described being in and out of Shock the rest of that summer. During what should have been a joyful time, they hid themselves away, avoiding having pictures taken, and stopped taking care of themselves. But there was no hiding their body from themselves, and slowly, over a period of months, they benefited from the tools of Exposure and Repetition in their own way: by getting tattoos to symbolize their transition. Now when they looked in the mirror, instead of focusing on their body or chest, their eyes were drawn instead to the art on their body.

As well as being William's way of taking ownership of their new body and how they were perceived in the world, getting tattoos allowed them to gaze at their body for longer without it triggering Shock. Every time the needle pulsated and filled in each pale patch of the soft new skin that had grown in with fresh, jet-black ink, William felt a bit more at home in this new body.

As William's story shows us, working through the Shock phase of Body Grief is not linear—and the path to Body Trust is not a perfect science. At any time during the journey, we can be plunged back into Shock in an instant as we come face-to-face with sobering realities. But I hope you are starting to realize just how important Shock is to the healing process overall.

Shock is what pulls our heads out of the haze and back into reality. It tells us that our Body Grief is real, that there is no going back, and that to heal we have no choice but to accept our body exactly where it's at. This truth may be scary, but it is empowering. Instead of it disavowing the reality of what we are experiencing, the acceptance that lies within Shock brings clarity and gives us back our power. If we can learn to stay in Shock long enough to acknowledge and even begin to accept our new reality, and if we can use what we learn in the process to begin to question our internalized beliefs about our body and our worth in the world, we will be on our way to building Body Trust. However, before we can arrive there, we must address the phase of Body Grief that often finds us as we emerge from Shock: Apology.

AFFIRMATIONS

"I am safe."

"I am deserving of ease."

"I am worthy and valued exactly as I am."

"I can sit in this discomfort and survive."

JOURNAL PROMPT

Write a letter to your past self, reflecting on your experiences of Shock with and in your body. Do you think your past self would be in Shock to learn of what you have been through?

FIVE

Apology:
Sorry for Being Me

After Emily learned that her pregnancy was not viable and that her body had not naturally miscarried after the standard five-day period, her doctor decided that medical intervention was necessary. She was given two options: medication, or a surgical procedure. Emily opted to take the at-home medicine. But it kicked in at an inopportune time, during a last-minute visit to see her sister-in-law Mandy and her kids.

Flushed from the long drive in, Emily walked carefully up the stairs to the bathroom, blood already dripping down her leg and through her shorts. Just a few weeks earlier, she'd had her wide-eyed son, almost a year old, happily and unknowingly hand her husband a book called *I Am Going to Be a Big Brother* with a positive pregnancy test inside. Her husband had looked directly at her, gobsmacked, and said, "We did this on our own, Em, but how?" They had assumed they would need to go back to the fertility clinic to get pregnant again, as they had with their firstborn, and hadn't bothered with birth control. And now this sweet surprise was leaving them.

The reality of what was happening hit Emily like an electric shock as she sat in her sister-in-law's clean, white-tiled bathroom as the medication kicked in. *How was this happening?* The feeling in her body was one of pure horror. But it was also tinged with relief that the waiting was over. Part of her knew this miscarriage needed to happen, despite the pain it caused.

From downstairs, the sound of her niece and nephew playing brought her back to her immediate reality. All of a sudden, all she could focus on was the mess she was making of her sister-in-law's bathroom. *Shit,* she thought. By now, her hands, legs, and clothes were covered in blood. She was going to have to clean everything up before she went downstairs and joined them. Emily snapped quickly into action, wiping the toilet seat and scrubbing the floor as she pushed aside the waves of sadness that threatened to overwhelm her. When she was done, she washed her hands and looked up at her reflection in the mirror. She felt completely separate from her body, almost not recognizing herself. "Don't make a fuss," she told herself. "You don't want to worry Mandy or scare the kids."

Emily put herself together as best she could and walked back downstairs. She had tried to return the bathroom to its previously pristine condition, but there was no hiding her bloodstained clothes. She pulled Mandy aside and in a quiet voice shared what had happened. As she finished, she saw tears well up in her sister-in-law's eyes. Immediately, Emily found herself wanting to console her. She felt terrible about bringing her mess and her Body Grief into Mandy's home; the last thing she wanted was to upset her family. "I am so, so sorry," she found herself repeating.

A miscarriage is perhaps one of the most visceral experiences of

Body Grief, because it results in the kind of loss that we most often associate with grief: the loss of another being. But even though Emily was devastated, the loss of her baby a fresh, deep wound in her body, all she could do was apologize, apologize for her Body Grief.

Apology: Our Attempt to Protect Ourselves and Others

The fourth phase of Body Grief, Apology, can be similar to Dismissal in that it may find us downplaying what we are experiencing. But where Dismissal's chief function is to protect us from facing what is happening, Apology, as we saw in Emily's story, is often about shielding others. Put another way, Apology can sound like "I'm sorry," but it can also sound like "It isn't that big of a deal" and "Don't mind me!" as we attempt to take up as little space as possible so as not to inconvenience others.

In this way, Apology also helps lessen our fear of being rejected for our perceived abnormalities and flaws. For example, if our Body Grief and what has triggered it feels like too much for us to contemplate and digest, then of course it must be too much for others. As humans, our fear of being rejected and not fitting in is primal. In fact, when we are faced with a threat—in this case, the overwhelming pain, frustration, and sadness of our Body Grief—adrenaline kicks into our central nervous system to help us either rage against what is happening (Fight, a phase we'll get to in chapter 7), flee or run from it (Dismissal), or freeze, making ourselves as small and quiet as possible in the hope that the threat will just go away. But with fawning, we try to avoid this danger and distress by people-pleasing, overcompensating, and, of course, apologizing.

Apology's other function shows up here, which is to help us self-regulate and dial down our emotional response to the Shock phase of our Body Grief. Emily's pregnancy loss triggered significant Body Grief for her, but following the Shock of what was happening, she almost immediately jumped to Apology. The thought of causing a ruckus or upsetting her sister-in-law was an easier problem to confront than her pain about the miscarriage itself. Therefore, her Apology became a means of self-regulating her central nervous system in a moment of pure Body Grief.

But while Apology provides a convenient and socially acceptable out from feeling our feelings in the moment, it doesn't actually lessen the pain of our Body Grief. Emily's loss was not suddenly any less devastating because she decided to focus on her sister-in-law's feelings or the mess she made in the bathroom. The cognitive dissonance of Apology—when we say or do one thing but think or feel something else—can be very diminishing to our ultimate trust in our bodies. This makes Apology one of the more toxic phases of the Body Grief process. When we belittle what we are going through, we are essentially telling our body, "You are not allowed to feel what you feel and need what you need. You don't matter." As always, the only way for Emily to process her true feelings about her miscarriage is to learn ways to accept and be with her Body Grief. This is true for all of us.

SIGNS YOU ARE IN APOLOGY

Apology can manifest in disclaimers you make for your body and its needs, and usually comes across as being polite, kind, and considerate, when in reality you may be experiencing significant physical and emotional pain. Perhaps you have excused your Body Grief with statements like "Sorry, I just had a baby," "Sorry, I ate too much on vacation," or "Sorry, I'm on medication." Or you've apologized for your weight gain, how your long illness or chronic condition means you're not able to go out most weekends, staying in bed during a depressive episode, needing to turn up the AC due to menopause symptoms, not having a drink with dinner because you're trying to quit alcohol, or needing to make adjustments to your order because you have a food intolerance.

You might also be in Apology if you find yourself constantly altering your reality to accommodate someone else's expectations. For example, you end up going to that work dinner despite having been up all night breastfeeding, because you feel you need to save face. You don't want to make a fuss in the rideshare, so you don't speak up when the seat belts won't fit over your plus-size belly. You attempt to get out of your wheelchair and walk upstairs to meet your friends at a restaurant that is not accessible. For while Apology can manifest in literally telling others that we are sorry for inconveniencing them, it can also look like removing ourselves from certain situations, not sharing what's really going on for us, making assumptions about how others will react to our situation, shrinking ourselves to take up less space, and masking our true experience to fit in.

Next time you find yourself either apologizing for your body and its needs or twisting yourself into knots as you try not to take up too much space, ask yourself: Am I making these accommodations to make *me* more comfortable, or to make *others* more comfortable with me? Given how many of us identify as people pleasers, chances are it's usually a bit of both. As we've seen, easing others' discomfort can be regulating for us, too. But as humans, we are allowed to have needs, and not everybody's needs are equal.

Somewhere in our upbringing, many of us were led to believe that our needs are part of a big accounting system in the sky, where somebody or something is keeping score. But I'm here to tell you: *no one is keeping score.* Your needs, no matter how outsized or outside of what is considered normal they may be, are just as important as everybody else's. Some people may never need the same level and specific kinds of care, assistance, and support that you do—and that's okay. There is, of course, a place for Apology in our lives: it is on us to apologize when our actions have hurt somebody. But apologizing for our Body Grief hinders our healing because it means saying sorry for something we have no control over.

How Perfectionism and Shame Fuel Apology

"Stop saying you're sorry, it's so annoying!"

I'll never forget my childhood friend saying this to me after I apologized for sneezing for the second time in a row. There was kindness in her eyes, but the words were so sharp off her tongue they left me paralyzed. What does a chronic people pleaser say to that if they can't say sorry?

I went home that day and told my mom what had happened. I remember being so sad; I didn't understand what was wrong with wanting to make others around me happy. Mom said we could work on it together. But looking back, I'm sure she was grateful to my friend for saying something, because back then, all I did was apologize. Once I started going through puberty, with all the Body Grief that came with this tumultuous phase in my life, it was like a switch went off. My body and its shifting needs felt too big and too loud, and I was mortified about just being me.

Enter the twin evils of perfectionism and shame: two of the core drivers of Apology, and two tenets of white supremacy, might I add! Perfectionism is often misunderstood as applying only to type A individuals who strive to get everything right. But we are all impacted by the perfectionist ideals of capitalism, white supremacy, and ableism, which, as we've learned, dictate that we must look, perform, and behave in a certain way in order to be considered valuable members of society. And because none of us are perfect, our perceived flaws can cause us to feel shame. Apologizing becomes our attempt to lessen this shame.

This is why, sadly, Apology is more common among women, who are often socialized not to take up too much space or make unreasonable demands. In this phase, we often apologize for what we see as our flaws and the "inconveniences" they cause, believing this will show that we are being considerate of others' needs—and that this in turn will make us more lovable. What's really happening? Internalized ableism and sexism are running the show.

We also see shame at play in sneaky ways within some in the disability community who use outdated terms such as "special needs," "differently abled," and "handi-capable." While intended to be inclusive, these labels assume that nondisabled people's abilities are "normal." Avoiding naming disability for what it is comes from a place of shame. Being disabled is an identity marker that is now being owned with pride by disabled folx who'd rather embrace their realities than ask to be seen as special or different compared to the non-disabled ideal normal. This new framing shows that disability *is* the norm for some of us—and nothing to be ashamed of.

In the same way, shame and internalized ableism fuel Apology in those of us with invisible illnesses and disabilities, such as autoimmune diseases, long COVID, mental illness, and even things like strep throat and the common cold. For example, Meredith, who lives with the invisible disability of hearing loss, found herself apologizing over and over again on a call to a travel agent as she attempted to adjust a reservation for a trip she and her fiancé were taking that month.

Listening from the other room, her fiancé overheard the script he knew all too well: "I'm sorry, I can't hear you. I'm sorry, can you please speak up? I'm sorry, can you please speak slower? I'm sorry, can you please repeat yourself?" As a seasoned therapist, Meredith has all the compassion in the world for others. She, with an alphabet of qualifications to her name and years of hard personal and professional work behind her, knows that she does not owe anyone an apology for why it is hard for her to hear them, especially if they start to become unkind. And yet, her internalized ableism and shame found her apologizing for her hearing loss yet again.

For Meredith, Apology is the result of feeling as if she owes the world an explanation for why she is the way she is, for having needs and for asking others to accommodate them. Because needs take up space, our instinct when we perceive them as being "too much" is to gather our needs up and pull them close, bottle them up, and apologize for said needs, as if we are apologizing for our mere existence. In Meredith's case, this happens multiple times per day at the checkout line, the grocery store, the movie theater, or just in passing. She describes each time she apologizes versus asking others to meet her where she's at as "small moments of lost connection." For every joke where she misses the punch line, and for every whisper where she misses the secret, she misses an opportunity to connect with another human being.

To many people, Meredith seems too young to be hard of hearing, deafness being something we may see as normal in older adults, and therefore deserving of making allowances. This means that both her shame and her Apology are rooted in ageism—something that often goes hand in hand with ableism.

But if we're lucky, we can all expect to grow old. And as we've learned, although society stubbornly refuses to accept disability as "normal," the disabled population is the only minority that everyone has a chance of becoming part of one day. In fact, loss of ability is a normal part of aging. This is why both ageism and ableism are two of the most insidious isms—we know we are *all* susceptible to them, and our fear of contagion makes it even harder for us to accept both aging and loss of ability as a normal part of life. When our turn inevitably comes, and with it Body Grief, the burden is on us to ensure that nobody else has to be confronted with the reality that one day it will be them. And in swoops Apology again.

Reflection

What memories have surfaced for you so far in this chapter? At what times in your Body Grief journey have you felt the need to apologize for being you? Have you ever downplayed what you are experiencing in your body? Has society told you not to be so loud, or that your needs were too much? Bring to mind a specific scenario in which you found yourself apologizing to avoid feeling the full force of your Body Grief. What experience led to this? How did your apology sound? What actions did you take? Apology can feel like hiding from ourselves, so it may be difficult to pinpoint times you have been in Apology, let alone what prompted it. Extend grace to yourself as you reflect on these moments and remind yourself that it is all part of the process.

I'm *Not* Sorry for Being Me: Moving through Apology

The first step to moving through Apology is to notice each instance of it as it manifests, then remind yourself that you are allowed to take up space and be unapologetically yourself. For example, if I feel I am "too much" for someone, I think, *They must be on some kind of diet, and I don't subscribe to diets anymore!* By refraining from apologizing or feeling like you must put others' comfort and needs before your own, you show yourself that it is okay to be *you*—and that there is nothing wrong with you for being wherever you are at with your body and Body Grief. From here, you can start to learn that your true value lies outside of your body.

As I learned to live with my condition, I continued to find myself always apologizing for something: my lack of mobility, the extra space my mobility aids took up, how damn slow I had gotten, my inability to participate in inaccessible places, my chair, my mobility service dog, even the time it took for me to get from my car to a restaurant. There was no more "running to the store" or "hopping in the shower" for me. I needed others to help me do the simplest things. But it just felt like too much to ask others to adjust on my behalf, and I was oh-so-very apologetic about being such a burden.

The first time I was able to overcome this was a game-changer for me. I had moved from Jackson Hole, Wyoming, to Charleston at age twenty-five and hadn't been home in a while. There were lots of reasons for this, but the changes to my body due to the brain and spine surgeries I had undergone, coupled with the restrictions of the pandemic, made it much harder to travel. This was heartbreaking, and my mom coming to visit me regularly felt like the only option we had. It was on one of these trips that she asked if I would be home that summer. I froze. We were sitting in the sun on my back porch. I didn't want to hurt her feelings, but I knew that I had to be honest.

"I want more than anything to come home and visit, Mom," I told her, my eyes starting to well up with tears. I tilted my head back so they wouldn't fall down my cheeks. "But the house is not accessible. I can't walk up and down the stairs. It's just too dangerous, and I know it worries you all, too."

I expected her to be hurt, or even get defensive. I didn't want to inconvenience my family or be a burden on them. But instead, she replied immediately, "Well, maybe we should get a stair lift!"

My eyes lit up. I couldn't believe what I was hearing. That was a big offer! Stair lifts could be pretty expensive; between the equipment and installation they might have to take out a loan to pay for this! Plus, they would have to sacrifice the aesthetic of their home. I knew the implications of this ask, as I, too, had recently become a homeowner. In my case, my community had really come through and built me a ramp so that I could access my own single-story home.

"Really? You would do that?" I asked.

She smiled. "Of course. Anything for our kids."

And that was that. Within a month, the stair lift had been installed, and I made my first trip home in years shortly after that. The lift made everything so much easier, and its presence in their home meant my parents continued to grieve with me in *our* Body Grief.

Let's take a look at some accessible strategies to help us move through this phase of Apology.

Tap into Your Apology

Wading into the Ocean of Body Awareness, let's tap into how it feels to be in Apology. Imagine trying to make yourself as small as possible and doing your best not to inconvenience anybody. How does this feel in your body? Clammy hands, a racing heart, a tight chest, and a stomach twisting into knots are common physical feelings triggered by feeling burdensome. Observe where in your body the urge to apologize comes from, and what happens when you do not act on it. What are you forced to feel?

Now open your heart to the idea that you are allowed to need whatever you need, and that these needs are allowed to expand and stretch out. How does it feel for your body and its needs to take up that much space? What sensations come up for you in your body now, and where?

Ask your body what it needs to take up all the time, space, and attention it needs for you to feel supported in your Body Grief. What does your body want you to know?

TAKE UP SPACE

Giving ourselves permission to take up space, as I did, creates the opposite of Apology: forgiveness—which in turn leads to freedom in our body. Even if it meant incurring major costs and inconvenience, me being honest about my mobility needs gave my mom the opportunity to get her need—to spend time with her daughter—met. Of course, not everybody will be in a position to physically alter their home in this way. Another solution would have been for my parents to accept that they would have to keep making the trip to see me and stop asking when I would be coming home. Or they could have set up an air bed on the ground floor, so I didn't have to take the stairs. Allowing ourselves to be as big and messy and inconvenient as we need to be is key to moving through this phase.

Let's go back to Emily's story for a minute. I recognize miscarriage is a heavy topic, and I am right here, feeling all the feelings with you. Sadly, Emily would experience a second pregnancy loss a year after that horrific afternoon at her sister-in-law's. But this time, she refused to let Apology stifle her Body Grief and instead allowed herself to ask for the support that she needed.

Emily remembers sitting in the lobby of the ob-gyn's office for what felt like over an hour the day she went in for her eight-week ultrasound, and then waiting another half hour, half naked with her legs in stirrups, for the doctor to see her. Finally, the technician came in, all smiles. But Emily knew exactly what to look and listen for. The tech's dark, deafening silence as she moved the sensor over Emily's belly told her everything she needed to know. There was no heartbeat, not even a flicker.

Emily felt her own heart breaking in that moment: *This is Body Grief.* But she quickly pushed the thought away and instead focused on how awful it must be for the tech to have to deliver the bad news. She waited for her to say something, anything. Why wasn't the tech saying anything? Emily felt anger rising in her but immediately excused the tech for her lack of empathy. *She must have a script she has to go by,* she thought. *This has to be so hard for her as well; she is measuring her response. How awful to have to give somebody this news.*

After a while, Emily finally broke the silence, asking the tech if she was still looking for the heartbeat. She replied that she was trying. Emily, in desperation, mustered up the words "Can you try again?" The tech apologized and said that she would be back. A few minutes later, the doctor entered the room and started to spit out medical jargon from behind a scripted veil of compassion. Emily was right: she had lost the baby again.

Before she got dressed, Emily held back tears as she tried her best to wipe off the remaining lubricant from the ultrasound. She felt terrible, but not totally for herself: the tech had been so happy to see her, and she'd ruined the tech's day. She took a deep breath and walked out of the exam room, where she was met with sad faces and sorrowful goodbyes. Emily felt as though she had to apologize for her own Body Grief yet again, when all she wanted to do was scream and rage at the unfairness of her situation, wanted to fall to the ground, cry, and be held. To feel the full force of her grief at losing a second pregnancy. Instead, she placed a hand on her heart, bowed her head, and whispered a demure thank-you to the receptionist as she left the clinic. But part of her knew that her Apology wasn't sustainable. Her body was playing by different rules now. She had shared it with her first child, and now with two more. She had to honor these losses.

In the parking lot, Emily settled into her car and called her husband. She told him everything, and to her surprise, he started to cry. For the first time, it felt like they were sharing the grief, and Emily started to feel her defenses settle, her grip on her composure loosen. *Of course* he was crying. *Of course* she was in so much pain it felt like a natural disaster was happening in her body. The Body Grief was all consuming.

She drove home shakily, holding back tears of her own, and when she opened the door, there was her sister-in-law, who had shown up for her unprompted. Emily crumpled into her arms and wept. As she sobbed and sobbed, lying down on the couch when she could no longer stand, she could almost feel the cortisol that had been holding her frozen in her fawn response ebbing from her body. She was able to finally feel, although it was so, so painful. As she rocked back and forth, her sister-in-law held her, and they felt the despair together. When her husband came home, they embraced and shared in their Body Grief. No apology was needed, no disclaimer. It was all allowed.

Emily finally allowed herself to take up space in her Body Grief. For you, taking up space may start with setting a boundary. A simple no to any request that makes you uncomfortable or is beyond your capability can be a deceptively powerful tool that helps you take up more emotional space than you are used to. It may mean voicing a vulnerable yes to help that you do not think you have a right to receive. It may also look like asking for help in the first place.

In our daily lives, taking up space can also look like dancing, wearing brighter colors and bolder clothes, rocking unique hairstyles, being authentically us, eating foods that we actually want, nourishing our body, and allowing it to expand. Remember, it is very natural to slip into Apology when we fear being seen as "too much." Simply being seen can feel very unsafe, depending on our level of privilege in this world. But if we practice being seen in other aspects of our life, it gets easier to remain visible in the throes of our Body Grief.

Exercise:

YELL IT OUT

Let's literally take up some space. Find a place that is safe, that is yours, and where you have no distractions. If you are home, it is okay to tell your family that you are doing an exercise and not to disturb you. You can also go into your car or find a secluded place in nature.

To begin, take a full, deep breath through your nose, hold at the top to allow the oxygen to flow to your brain, and then exhale audibly through the mouth. Shake your hands if you can and repeat, inhaling fully through the nose, holding briefly at the top, and then exhaling loudly. Do this about five times until it becomes natural for you.

Now, I want you to think about all of your needs, all of the ways in which you have apologized for your Body Grief lately. Where in your body can you feel that grief right now? Deep in your gut? In the back of your throat? Between your toes? Where is it? Let's give it a voice. Focus on the sensation and keep breathing, and then spread your body out as much as you are physically able. Stretch out your fingers, toes, arms, and legs. Open your mouth wide and stick out your tongue. Make your body as long and wide as you possibly can. Make yourself big. Take up space!

Now, with everything you've got, scream, yell, yodel, and get loud. Feel the sensations of your Body Grief leaving your body. At first, this may feel incredibly odd and uncomfortable, even scary, but each time you do this exercise it will feel more empowering. Return to this whenever you are stuck in Apology and need to make space for your Body Grief.

THESE ARE MY PEOPLE: FIND COMMUNITY IN YOUR BODY GRIEF

Being in a community with individuals who can relate to your Body Grief experiences can be another powerful remedy for Apology. Following her second miscarriage, Emily found that joining Facebook groups and sharing her miscarriage journey on social media helped her feel less isolated and alone. Hearing from others who had also grappled with the Body Grief of pregnancy loss showed her that it was indeed "normal" to be feeling the way she was feeling, and to need what she needed to heal.

In a society that celebrates independence and individualism, it can be easy to forget how much we truly need other people. We tend to think about community in terms of our family, friend groups, work colleagues, and educational and religious groups: in other words, the people who are *there*. And they are absolutely essential to moving through Apology. But it is also helpful to, like Emily, find spaces where we can commune with others who are also on the Body Grief journey and can bring a sense of solidarity, support, and acknowledgment.

For example, traditional grief circles allow those who are mourning the loss of a loved one the space to grieve, heal, and discover who they are becoming now that their loved one has passed on. This is true for Body Grief, too. These groups may not be marketed as such, but recovery circles, writing groups, painting classes, yoga classes, and other healing practices can offer diverse people with similar interests a potential place to come together in their Body Grief. Knowing that everybody in the room has likely had similar experiences and felt similar things as us is a relief—we don't have to pretend to have it all together anymore!

But how do you find community to support you in your Body Grief? The first step is finding a group that is bonded by a common interest. You can search online. Local libraries often offer a wealth of in-person resources. And as the wonderful Issa Rae said in an interview once, if something doesn't already exist, why not create it? This is where the power of social media comes in. Simply creating a page dedicated to your area of interest can immediately help you find others who are in the same boat—whether in an online chat room, a local painting group, or a monthly gathering for local activists, the opportunities are endless.

From there, moving through Apology in community means allowing yourself to be vulnerable with others, lowering your mask of decorum, and being real about what you're going through—then doing your part by continuing to show up and witness others in their Body Grief.

REFRAME APOLOGY WITH
COGNITIVE BEHAVIORAL THERAPY

Cognitive behavioral therapy (CBT) is another tool that can help you move through Apology. A super-accessible form of therapy, CBT works by separating our thoughts from our feelings, and our feelings from our behaviors. The theory is that every maladaptive behavior starts with an activating event, and that this event leads to a cognitive distortion that creates a feeling and leads to a specific behavior. CBT helps you reframe those initial cognitive distortions to alter how you feel, which in turn allows you to choose a different behavior.

For example, you share a picture of yourself online for the first time in a while after having gained weight (activating event) and feel the need to explain or apologize for this change in your body. The thoughts accompanying this might be, *Ugh, I hate my body. I hate how it looks in this photo. Nobody will love me like this* (cognitive distortion). This manifests in anxiety, disgust, self-hate, and fear of rejection (feelings), which leads to extreme dieting or purging (behavior), sparking a bout of Body Grief. Apology in this case might sound like "I am too much. I am sorry for taking up this space both emotionally and physically. I must fix this problem. I must make myself smaller." Internally, the unspoken impulse behind the Apology is *I need to regulate this feeling.*

To work through Apology using CBT and to take up space, you would start by reframing these self-hating thoughts: *This is my body today, and this photo captures more than my weight. It captures joy and memories, which is why I want to share it with the world.* Or perhaps: *I do not owe the world any explanation for my appearance. My worth and value lie in my connections and memories, which is why I am posting this photo.*

Can you already feel in your body how this leads to less anxiety and begins to generate feelings of self-acceptance? Over time, repeatedly reframing our thoughts in this way ultimately creates new neural pathways and ways of thinking. The goal within CBT is to feel slightly less activated, reduce unease, and generate feelings of confidence until, eventually, there is no need to apologize for anything.

"Who I Am Is Just Right": Eric's Story

To close us out, let's look at how someone might use all three of these tools—taking up space, community, and CBT—to move past Apology and toward Body Trust. Eric was raised in a traditional and very conservative Roman Catholic Hispanic household where, as somebody who identifies as queer and nonbinary, they experienced significant emotional and physical abuse.

"I remember being told that who I am is fundamentally undesirable to God, the creator of the universe. That me—who I am, not what I do—is wrong, a sin, an abomination," they said. Understandably, this resulted in an adolescence and early adulthood marked by self-abandonment and Body Grief. Eric felt that they could not let anyone know who they were, or risk being seen, for fear of being rejected or even physically harmed. Although they were completely confident in who they were, describing their orientation as a "chemical equation that was with/in my body," they asked themselves, "What is the point of growing up and trying to be here if I'm going to burn in hell anyways?" This was the seed of the Eric's Body Grief—which they have reframed as Queer Grief.

Eric began apologizing for who they are at age ten, when they began starving themselves out of existence. Following their eating disorder recovery at age eighteen, they found a new way to disappear: into addiction to substances. This coincided with them coming out as queer.

"You can argue that the world is more open-minded, but the same violence was just lurking in different corners, coming out of different mouths, and moving through different vehicles," they told me. "I was terrified, and the way in which I embodied being a queer person felt like it was too much."

Immersing themselves in the party culture, Eric soon discovered that cocaine numbed the anxiety and fear of their Body Grief. It felt like a solution. All of a sudden, they didn't care what their voice sounded like, how they moved through the world, or what people thought of them. Their Body Grief was still there, but it hurt less. The numbing effect of the drugs was incredibly seductive—but their "fabulous" exterior was just another apology for who they *really* were.

Eric couldn't see this until they were deep in their recovery from substance use, crying on the bathroom floor in the fetal position, snot bubbling from their nostrils, and mascara running down their face: this was their Apology finally leaving their Body. In that moment, they were done saying sorry for who they were. Doing so took too much from them. Taking up space meant feeling all the feelings they had been avoiding by not eating and by getting high: the anger, the violation of their body and soul, the rejection of self, and the self-hatred. Instead of starving it, snorting it, smoking it, and screwing it away, it was time to let their terrified, traumatized ten-year-old self be seen and heard.

The process of being seen continued with finding community in twelve-step recovery spaces, where Eric learned that it was okay to take up space with their messy, confusing, and painful experiences of Queer Body Grief. In recovery, Eric was also able to reframe their concept of God, and to reclaim their relationship with a higher power who loves them. Today, God is nothing but love to them; if any God others rather than loves, then it is just another instrument of disease and shame.

Eventually, Eric took on a sponsor role and became a vocal and highly visible advocate in the LGBTQ+ recovery space. In addition, they began working with a therapist on CBT techniques to change the channel whenever their thought patterns got stuck in the cognitive distortions that had led them down a path of self-diminishing (and in their case, potentially life-threatening) Apology. Now when Eric starts thinking, *No one is going to love me if I sound like that* and *I'm just too much*, they stop and say, "There I go again!" to lovingly stop the Apology in its tracks. Using the CBT skills they have learned, they reframe the thought as *It is homophobia and other systems of oppression that make me feel like I am "too much." I have so much to give to this world in my authentic embodied self!*

Both Eric's and Emily's stories show us the power of taking up space and reframing our thoughts to help us notice when we are in Apology and move through this necessary and unavoidable phase of the Body Grief process. Finding a community where we feel safe to be seen and heard in all of our messy, confusing, and inconvenient needs can help us work through significant grievances, from pregnancy loss, Queer Body Grief, and systemic injustices to maladaptive coping mechanisms like substance use and eating disorders. The key to moving past Apology is to find ways to allow ourselves to spread out both physically and emotionally, no disclaimers needed. But what can find us on the other side of Apology is a need to place the blame for our condition somewhere—and that place is often ourselves. And so we enter the fourth phase of Body Grief: Fault.

AFFIRMATIONS

"Right now, it is like this."

"I am uncomfortable with my body in this moment, and that is okay."

"I am working on trusting my body."

"I do not need to apologize for what I am experiencing."

JOURNAL PROMPT

Free-write on the following prompt for five to ten minutes: "It is not my job to apologize for . . ."

SIX

Fault: Playing the
Blame Game

⌒

Michelle was nine years old when her mom told her to stay off
the monkey bars at the local jungle gym. She had always
loved playing on them, the way the tendrils of hair from her half-up,
half-down ponytail shielded her eyes as she swung from one rung to
the next, arms going slightly numb as she pushed herself to make it
all the way across before landing both feet triumphantly in the freshly
laid mulch. But now those days were behind her.

"It's time to act how you look, not your age," her mom admon-
ished. It was her attempt to prepare her daughter for a life of being hypersexualized due to her rapidly developing body. Having
been raised in a traditional, uber-patriarchal, conservative Christian
home, for Michelle's mother, being a woman, especially a Black and
Latina woman, meant being both objectified and shamed for simply
being in a body. With her mom as her chaperone, Michelle now had

to sit the monkey bars out, watching her friends swing from bar to bar as she did her best to become as small and inconspicuous as possible. Afraid that the dads, older brothers, and other men at the playground would be "tempted" by her developing womanly curves, she sat with her legs crossed, arms folded over her chest.

"My mom was the first person to tell me that I was sexy," she later told me. "I think she was trying to protect me, but it ricocheted as shame and hurt me in the process." Not only could Michelle no longer have fun at the jungle gym, but she no longer felt safe in her body. It was too "developed," too "showy." She was reminded of this constantly by her mom, who she knew was trying to protect her. But her mother's fears were confirmed by the stares she had started to get from older men in the park. The result was a loss of innocence and a loss of freedom. It was as if her body had betrayed her.

A year later, Michelle had an experience that would confirm her mother's worst fears, compounding her Body Grief. A couple of girls who were a few grades above her came over for a playdate. Michelle's mom was in the military, and the family lived on base. That night, her mom was working a late shift and her father, who was home after coaching basketball, was in charge—and the girls molested Michelle. She remembers feeling confused, thinking, "This must be how we play," but then feeling scared and full of shame. She thought her dad had seen what happened, but he never mentioned it. In the weeks, months, and years that followed, the only way Michelle could make sense of that night was to blame herself. She had been violated because of how "sexy" her body was. *Act how you look, not your age.* Maybe this was how you acted how you looked.

Years later during Christmas, her father finally shared that he had known all along about the incident. At the time, he'd written it off as kids being kids. His goal in sharing this now, he said, was to help Michelle feel seen. But Michelle didn't feel seen. She was furious, as the shame that had been weighing her down now turned to anger. Where was this validation when she had needed it at the time? Her anger was directed at her dad, the military, and the patriarchy in general for silencing her feelings and pushing the issue under the rug so as not to upset the status quo. It was directed at her mom for failing to teach her how to be safe without feeling ashamed of her biracial body in a society that hypersexualizes Black and Latina women. She was also angry at those girls, who she knew had also been exposed to sex at a very young age.

Michelle then realized she had never blamed them for what happened. Yes, her family, society, and the perpetrators themselves had all played a role. But when it came down to it, it had been easier for Michelle to believe that what had happened to her was all her body's fault.

Fault: The Search for Why

Fault is ever present when we grapple with the "why" and the "how the hell do I fix this?" of our Body Grief. When we're in Apology, we take on responsibility for holding and managing the pain, discomfort, and inconvenience of whatever is driving our Body Grief. We move into Fault when we begin to ask *why* we have been saddled with this burden.

At its root, Fault is a function of the flight part of the fight, flight, freeze, or fawn stress response. When we're looking for an answer to our Body Grief, we are searching for an escape from whatever madness is happening in our body. We believe that if we can find the problem, we can stop the pain and our suffering will end.

But diving even deeper, Fault stems from our very real and valid fear of sickness and pain, in each of its physical, mental, and emotional forms. Sickness and pain cue us to danger, even death. Seen this way, you can see how Fault stems from our most basic survival instinct.

This also makes Fault another place where "fear of contagion" rears its head. When confronted with someone who is ill, or disabled, or fat, or suffering a miscarriage, or in the throes of their Body Grief in whichever way it manifests, we silently ask ourselves, *What happened to you that you are like this?* But what we mean is *What can I do to prevent this awful thing from happening to me?* But finding something or someone to blame for a body not functioning the way we think it should—whether said body belongs to us or not—negates a simple truth: the human body is as fragile and as unpredictable as fuck. Sickness, disability, mental health issues, accidents, and assault can happen to *any of us* at *any time.* How absolutely terrifying.

This is why it is so common to find ourselves in Fault. Of course none of us wants to get hurt! It is also the reason Fault can become addicting, keeping us stuck in this phase long after it is helpful. On a subconscious level, finding what is to blame for our Body Grief feels like a life-or-death matter to us—we will not stop until we get an answer, until we are *safe.* But the answer to our condition is often not clear-cut, as is the case with many chronic illnesses and disabilities. With no obvious diagnosis and no way to make sense of what we're experiencing, we can experience a phenomenon known as "flare chasing": when our symptoms are in a "flare" we have tangible evidence in our hands, and the instinct can be to go on a mission to find the "source" for what caused the onset of said flare-up.

It is natural to want a reason for our pain and discomfort. Having a clear-cut explanation eases our anxiety and helps us feel like we are taking control over what may feel like an uncontrollable situation. If we can get to the root of whatever is causing our Body Grief, we think, we can undo what has happened. We can get back to how we were. But getting stuck in Fault can cause us to internalize a ton of resentment, blame, and shame. And it is all-too easy to find fault in ourselves, because we are often the only variable we believe we can control. *If only we had looked, acted, or chosen differently*, we believe, *none of this would have happened*.

This brings us back to Perceived Body Betrayal. Whatever we decide is at fault for our Body Grief, deep down we will likely find ourselves asking *why me?* The answer to which often becomes *because my body has betrayed me*. It is too weak, too defective, or just plain unlucky. We could equally feel betrayed by a body that is fat, queer, trans, Black, Brown, neurodivergent, or in any way different from the ideal normal. Whatever the reason, it is almost impossible not to turn the finger on ourselves—or even God, the universe, or whichever word you use for whatever keeps the earth spinning. If only we had just been born in a different body, in a different culture, at a different time, then none of this would be happening. At what point did we sign up for *this* body and *this* life?

The thing is, this thinking is incredibly self-shaming, and it can lead us to act out in toxic ways. In the case of Michelle's mother, because she had also been sexualized as a child, first becoming pregnant at age fifteen, all she wanted was to protect her daughter from experiencing the same. But it was easier for her to find fault with her daughter's developing body than it was to question or hold accountable the misogynistic, patriarchal culture she was raised in, and the male sexual entitlement it enables. Scolding Michelle for being "too sexy" was a maladaptive yet somewhat resourceful way for her mom to make sense of her own experiences. Her daughter's Body Grief was simply the collateral damage.

But when our Body Grief is the result of misogyny, racism, homophobia, transphobia, or whichever ism we grapple with, remember, the fault does not lie in you: it lies squarely with the way we are impacted by these systems of oppression. There is power in acknowledging this. Except for in the experience of living with actual physical pain, Body Grief *only exists* in relation to the way our body is perceived in society and how this impacts our choices and the way we are treated. For example, if a thin, white, nondisabled, straight, upper-middle-class man experienced early onset puberty like Michelle did, he would likely not experience the same shaming and sexualization, because his body would not be subject to the racism, misogyny, sexism, and fatphobia Michelle was subjected to.

This is deeply unfair, and I want to validate any trauma response that arises as you're reading this. It is very natural to feel anger about how the various isms have been created intentionally to give some people power over others. But in the end, it is not helpful to sit in Fault and expect our righteous rage to make our Body Grief go away. Fault is not a fix. It is what we *do* with this information that can give us power, and our anger about oppressive systems can become fuel for advocacy and activism. So get mad, feel all the feelings, then let's do something with that anger.

It's really hard not to point fingers when we are in pain, and ultimately Fault can help us feel better by making us feel more in control. Humans thrive on answers—once we know why something isn't working, we can look for a way to fix it. But the truth is, we are never in control. And while Fault *can* sometimes help us find immediate relief, in the best-case scenario, what it can do is show us where we must work to make peace with our body, our circumstances, our limitations, and our choices. The key to preventing Fault from becoming our toxic default response to our pain and suffering is to cultivate the mindset that no one thing is ever fully and solely to blame for how things are. Sometimes things *just are.*

SIGNS YOU ARE IN FAULT

Getting stuck in a loop of searching for answers as to *why* this—whatever "this" may be—is happening to you is the most obvious sign that you are in Fault.

I remember the night Fault found my husband and I up until two a.m., going down internet rabbit holes. One year into my chronic illness journey, my legs were getting weaker, my sight was worsening, and my pain was off the charts. Sitting there on our phones in the dark, we needed to know: *Why was this happening to me?* A lack of answers quickly morphed into me blaming myself. "What did I eat?" "What did I *not* do?" "Was it because of my eating disorder?" "Was my body just *broken?*"

This faultfinding is what makes it so easy to get stuck in this phase. Unless our Body Grief is clearly the result of a specific accident or injury, there often are no easy answers to questions like these—and even then it can be hard. So we go around in circles searching for something or someone to blame, often ending up right back at ourselves. As a result, we may become tense and guarded as we brood on our issues and feel untrusting of the world and its potentially harmful impact on us. We may get easily agitated and quick to anger. We can also start to feel as if we are holding a grudge—but against what, specifically, remains unclear.

At its root, Fault is fueled by an overall sense that something is "out to get us," even our own body. This in turn brings us right back to Perceived Body Betrayal and creates the opposite of Body Trust. We feel like we have failed when we cannot pinpoint the cause of our Body Grief, manifesting in shame and making us defensive. All of this makes Fault a very unsettling place to be, which can lead us to seek comfort in food, alcohol, drugs, and other dopamine-laced behaviors to override the uncomfortable feeling that your body, and the world, are somehow against you.

Reflection

Think of a specific time that you found yourself in Fault. What did that situation look like for you? As you reflect on all of this, remind yourself that it is totally okay to want answers for why you feel the way you do, and what you can do about it.

Most of the Time, There Is No "Fix" for Our Condition—and That's Okay

In the age of information overload, we are presented with endless options for where to put our blame for our lack of well-being—making it almost impossible to just accept our body where it is at and find peace in our Body Grief process.

For example, the #Wellness industry plays a huge role in keeping us stuck in the Fault phase with its promise of endless fixes for what it paints as the causes of our Body Grief: the gluten, the dairy, your limiting beliefs, even Mercury in retrograde. The message that something "out there" is to blame for your Body Grief, and that it is in your power to fix it, is also the foundation of the entire self-help paradigm. In fact, Fault is probably one of the things that led you to this book, which you likely picked up with hopes to heal or fix your Body Grief. I don't blame you for this one bit. But the reality is, we will never be able to heal every part of ourselves and arrive at a destination of pristine health, wellness, and recovery. Living in a body means experiencing pain, discomfort, and fear. Please run a mile from anything or anyone who tells you otherwise.

As we've been learning, living with our Body Grief is an ongoing, ever-evolving journey. It is nonlinear, multidimensional, forever a work in progress, and there is no way to fix it. Capitalism makes healing seem like it's something we can do or buy—when in reality, it's a multifaceted, highly individual process that happens over time. I wanted healing to be yoga poses, turmeric lattes, waterfalls, and naps. But it is pain, snot-bubbling meltdowns, and hard conversations with myself and others.

This quick-fix mindset is rooted, unsurprisingly, in internalized ableism. We want to find a reason for why we are "defective" or "not normal," but we forget there is no such thing as normal. Healthy, nondisabled humans assume that sick, disabled humans are defective due to ableist beliefs, *not* because there is anything inherently wrong with being sick or disabled. But when a person's body is seen as defective, for whatever reason, in swoops the urge to fix it, all wrapped up as Fault.

We've seen this in the rise of diagnoses and treatments for people who are deemed neurodivergent and living with ADHD or autism. For some neurodivergent folx, getting an official diagnosis is a function of Fault: now they have a name for why they are unable to perform like their neurotypical friends and colleagues. Perhaps there is even a medication they can take to "fix the problem." This can be hugely relieving! But had society placed different demands on them as individuals, such as teaching them that it was okay to learn and work at their own pace and in their own way, there would not be anything to "fix" in the first place. Instead, they might have learned to wear noise-canceling headphones when feeling overstimulated, or have been validated in spending time educating friends and family on what it means to be neurodivergent. In other words, it is ableist standards that make life harder for neurodivergent people—when, in fact, their brain is not broken, and there is no fixing to be done.

In our search for answers to our Body Grief, we might find that there are too many options. When this happens, we might begin living in fear, as if any choice we make could set us back or make us worse.

Reflection

The Fault phase of Body Grief is often targeted commercially by the #wellness industry. Being served endless ads for "miracle" weight-loss gummies, IG memes listing "ways to know if you're a narcissist," and supplements that promise to regrow hair, cure anxiety, and beat the bloat are all examples of this. In what ways has this dynamic impacted you? What quick fixes have you been sold, and what was the outcome of engaging with them?

VIVIENNE'S STORY: WHEN FINDING FAULT CREATES MORE BODY GRIEF

Vivienne, a past client of mine, had this exact experience. Complaining of bloating, GI issues, joint pain, depression, chronic fatigue, and anxiety, her symptoms were dismissed for years by her doctors. Eventually, Vivienne's family decided to try a different approach and paid out of pocket for her to see a holistic dietician.

Vivienne finally felt heard: her new doctor was taking the time to truly listen to her, with the goal of finding the "why" versus simply treating her symptoms. She was prescribed various lifestyle practices, including a new diet, and she was overjoyed to discover that she started to feel much better. Having been advised to cut out all processed foods, Vivienne was now eating exclusively organic, grain-free, dairy-free, pesticide-free, hormone-free, and GMO-free. But over time, this led to her severely restricting her diet and becoming obsessed about what she was allowed to eat. This in turn presented a new set of symptoms—adding a new layer to her Body Grief.

By the time I met Vivienne, her eyes were sunken, her hair was thinning, and she was utterly exhausted from keeping up with all the rules of her new regimen. She was having issues sleeping, her bones had become brittle, and her skin had an orange tinge due to malnutrition. Not to mention, she was consumed with anxiety about the cost of her weekly food bills and obsessed with monitoring every bite she ate for how it made her feel. As a result, her list of "allowed" or "safe" foods had dwindled—until she was hardly eating anything at all.

The lifestyle that was supposed to be making her feel better was completely unsustainable, and she was distraught: What was she supposed to do now? So I asked her, "Is this healthy to you?" She responded, "I felt so good for a while, and then I couldn't keep up, and now it's like I'm sick *because* I want to feel better." How ironic. In her desire to find what was to blame for her Body Grief, Vivienne had been prescribed an eating disorder.

I Am Not to Blame:
Moving through Fault

What I want you to remember, is that it is very normal to play the Blame Game and try to find what is at fault for your pain and suffering. You are only trying to make sense of the mess. That said, getting stuck in Fault can find us going around in circles, and inevitably winding up pointing the finger at the only thing we believe we can control: ourselves. Let's look at some tools for avoiding this trap, as we examine the role of healthy rage, how to keep our focus on "what next?," and the power of zooming out from our present circumstances to take in the big picture—all of which can help us keep moving through Fault.

THE ROLE OF HEALTHY RAGE

While Fault makes us believe we can become immune to Body Grief, remember, there is nothing we can do to change our biology, turn back time, or guarantee we will never experience suffering in our body. At this point in our Body Grief process, it can all feel so *unfair.* This in turn can trigger a lot of emotions, especially anger.

Anger gets a bad rap, but it can actually be very resourceful. When we know how to use it, anger can be the fuel to help us override Dismissal and advocate for ourselves and others. It can flip us out of Apology and help us take up space. Anger also tells us about how we feel in our relationships, especially our relationship with our body. It arises to show us where a line has been crossed, and where a need has gone unmet. Have we been setting good boundaries? Have we been fulfilling our wishes and desires? But unfortunately, most of us are taught that anger is bad, and that we must control it.

Growing up, whenever I got angry, I was told to go to my room and calm down. The same goes for my husband, Sean—even if he also learned that men are allowed to be angry under certain circumstances. For example, it's okay to scream at the television when there's a game on or take out aggression roughhousing with the guys. For women, however, anger is often simply not allowed. Because anger is seen as the preserve of men, in women and woman-identifying people, it is seen as them being crazy, bitchy, immature, and not feminine.

This double standard is also intersectional. For instance, Michelle and I spoke about the "angry Black woman" trope that paints Black women as being hostile and aggressive by nature. This oppressive stereotype dismisses the fact that Black women often have *a lot* to be angry about, and have often had to protect themselves and their families from a world in which being in a Black body means literally being in danger. By painting Black women as defective in their anger, they are not given permission to feel their very legitimate feelings of rage within a system that is rigged against them and their bodies.

A lot of the time, anger also doesn't feel good, and getting stuck in anger is a common fear. I see this among my clients, who often tell me, "I am terrified that if I let myself feel angry, I won't come out of it." Much like with other big emotions, being with the full force of anger can be scary. But when we repress our anger, it often comes out in unhelpful ways, as we turn it on innocent bystanders or direct it back toward ourselves. And when anger sees Fault turn to blame, it gnaws away at us from the inside, manifesting in resentment and shame.

In essence, anger is information: it shows us where we need to act. But when we use it as fuel to inflame our emotional pain, this can look like yelling, numbing with alcohol and other substances, emotional and physical abuse, depression, anxiety, and self-harm. When we get stuck in blame, we stay angry and resentful of our body in its grief, and even of life itself. And when we are angry at life, it is hard to find pockets of joy, or the small moments that tap us back into its beauty and mystery: the sun shining on my cat Lilly's belly as I sip my coffee on our magical back porch; the nostalgic harmonies of my favorite '90s boy band echoing through my humble home; watching reruns of *Gilmore Girls* on Netflix as I snuggle with my pup Giovanni;

laughing at silly stories with my sisters as we share a glass of wine; the smell of the marsh as the ocean breeze hits my sun-kissed shoulders. These moments help rescue us from getting bogged down in self-pity.

FROM "WHY ME?" TO "WHAT NOW?"

Anger can make us ask "Why me?" as if the whole world is conspiring against us in our Body Grief. But self-pity is a slippery slope and is often confused with allowing ourselves to be in our emotions. There's a big difference here. Being with our emotions means observing, recognizing, naming, feeling, and, most important, *moving through* them. Self-pity, on the other hand, is a symptom of victim mentality, as if life is happening *to* us rather than *with* us and *for* us.

As important as it is to understand that sometimes the game is indeed rigged, wallowing in self-pity can become addictive, causing us to ruminate on past and present hardships rather than accepting our current reality and acting in the present. There is so much power in learning to be with our Body Grief, rather than being a victim of our pain. For this reason, asking "What now?" instead of "Why me?" is the golden tool for moving through this phase of Body Grief.

Let's go back to Vivienne's story for a second. When we started working together, we began by detaching the concept of morality and value from food. No food is inherently good or bad, and no one is morally superior for eating or not eating a certain type of food. Vivienne's restricted diet meant her microbiome was also completely disrupted; therefore, as we introduced new foods into her diet, she would bloat and have a lot of stomach pain.

This would lead to bouts of flare chasing, where she would immediately dive back into her comfort zone of "let's restrict; that is how we will find the culprit." By doing this she was able to oh-so-slyly dissociate from her pain without even realizing she was doing it. Going through her food logs, marking down ingredients, googling macros, figuring out how fiber digests in the gut, was all a distraction from the truth: what she needed was to nourish her body and be patient.

When this happened, we worked to help her move from "Why?" to "What now?," which meant adopting what's called a harm reduction approach. Harm reduction is about finding a way to reduce discomfort while having compassion for what our body is telling us it needs right now. In Vivienne's case, instead of finding fault with the one ultimate culprit for what she was feeling and eradicating it from her diet, I encouraged her to use self-care tools such as a heating pad, aromatherapy, breath work, and abdominal stretches to ease her discomfort in the moment. None of these tools would be a clear-cut fix. But they helped reduce Vivienne's pain, allowing her to move more easily through Fault and stay with her Body Grief.

I encourage you to ask yourself "What now?" anytime you find yourself in Fault. These two words can truly feel like a breath of fresh air, releasing you from worry and guilt, and freeing you from needing to know the why. What might this look like for you? Let's say you've been struggling with keeping focus lately. You're not quite sure what's going on, but it's been causing a lot of Body Grief and today it tipped you over the edge. On your way to work you not only spilled your coffee all over your blouse, but you arrived late for a meeting. Then your kid called you complaining that you forgot to pack them a lunch.

Rather than trying to figure out what's wrong with you, this is where I would encourage you to slow down and simply ask yourself "What now?" Because right now is the time to take care of you. "What now?" may look like texting a friend to drop off lunch for your kiddo or sending them cash to pick something up if you are able. It might mean taking a moment to breathe and give yourself some love and compassion, throwing on a sweater to cover the coffee stain, and moving some things off your calendar. Yes, there likely is something going on under the surface—but the "why" can wait for now. Tomorrow, "what now" might look like making an appointment with your primary care doctor. The key is to always give your body what it needs today as you take it one step at a time.

ZOOMING OUT: THE POWER OF A BIG-PICTURE PERSPECTIVE

There are still days when I fall into self-pity (I mean, who wouldn't?). But most days, I am able to lean into the perspective that life is bigger than me, that I am truly just along for the ride. I call this Zooming Out: finding your higher purpose and trusting in something bigger than your pain.

For some, this may look like practicing religion or having faith in a universal grand plan. For others, it may be tapping into creative outlets, connections with friends, charity work, parenting and caregiving, or working with animals. Whatever you find works for you, Zooming Out to take in the big picture can help alleviate our immediate pain and cultivate gratitude, putting our Body Grief into perspective as we gently move from "Why me?" to "What now?"

The truth is, our Body Grief cannot be solved. The more we can accept this, the closer we come to Body Neutrality and Body Peace. For this reason, managing our expectations is in fact part of the healing process, as it helps us connect with our body in the moment, wherever it is at. In this, we grant ourselves permission to let go of "getting better" and lean into "This is where I am at; what do I need right now?" This approach is rooted in kindness and compassion, a powerful antidote for whenever we find ourselves caught in an obsessive, toxic loop of Fault and self-pity.

Exercise:

ASK "WHAT NOW?"

Think of a time you experienced Fault in your Body Grief and asked yourself, "Why me?" Remember, it is *not* fair that you experienced or are experiencing this, and it's okay to feel mad. Now let's look at a couple of ways to flip into a "What now?" mindset. Think of five to ten things that would help you feel better right now, without having to "fix" what you are experiencing. For example, if you are experiencing chronic neck pain, those things may be:

1. Heating pad

2. Meditation

3. Neck brace

4. CBD balm

5. Medication

6. Rest

7. FaceTime with friend

8. Calming playlist

"I Am Exactly Where I Am Supposed to Be": Marka's Story

My friend Marka has every right to ask "Why me?" when it comes to the sheer amount of pain and suffering she has experienced in her body. But her ability to be and stay with her Body Grief, and to practice Body Trust using a zoomed-out perspective while consistently working to move from "Why me?" to "What now?" makes her one of my ultimate Body Grief role models.

Now in her sixties, Marka moved to Argentina to pursue a career as a ballerina when she was twenty-three. But she was forced to make the difficult decision to return to the States after her infant son was born with a rare genetic defect, a condition that would require a level of health insurance coverage that was believed to be better in the States. So Marka moved back to Charleston, South Carolina, as a single mom, changed careers, and became a full-time firefighter and EMT. To her surprise, she loved it: "It was like playing a role in the theater. We had costume changes, daily movement, even choreography that we needed to memorize. It wasn't so different from being a dancer!" Three years into her role, however, a stretcher she was holding broke, resulting in a spinal cord injury from the whiplash that was the equivalent of having been hit by a car traveling at 50 mph.

Forced to retire from her job, Marka worked tirelessly in spinal cord rehabilitation, eventually going back to work part time. Trying to find a purpose in it all, she also began teaching an adaptive ballet and yoga class at the hospital wellness center. She was heading home from class one day when a car ran a red light at a high speed and T-boned Marka in the driver's door. This accident resulted in a second spinal cord injury that left her paralyzed and immobile from the shoulders down. It was not long after that she underwent a full hysterectomy due to excessive bleeding from tumors in her uterus, as well as received a breast cancer diagnosis. How could this warrior of a woman not find herself asking *Why me?!*

Shame sat heavy on Marka like a cloak as others would also ask, "Why you?" What she internalized was "There must be something wrong with you to deserve all this!" But she would put on a "brave, pretty face," channeling her inner performer and masking her shame, which, left unprocessed, eventually morphed into anger and blame.

Given all she experienced, Marka could have spent her whole life in Fault, and she has certainly spent time here. "Initially, I blamed the US health insurance system, then I blamed the guy that dropped the stretcher, and then I blamed the driver that ran the red light," she said. "Fault and anger built over time. I knew it wasn't rational. These things were accidents, and there was nothing I could have done to prevent getting sick. And yet there were times I couldn't stop myself from going there."

She describes sitting in the courtroom with her latest set of injuries, her body almost completely paralyzed, while the woman who hit her car was given a $150 ticket. It was like being hit all over again, but no one was coming to save her this time. The dull ache in her body was building, and it wasn't just her nerve pain that was her daily companion—it was the heavy pain of resentment, a pain that went beyond the physical and felt like it was crushing her spirit. In the courtroom, shifting from "Why me?" to "What now?" meant changing her perspective: "I didn't want to be angry at the world, or at that girl. She was young and in a hurry, just trying to get to her job."

Ultimately, Marka has learned that staying in Fault only hurts her. When she was diagnosed with breast cancer two years after her second accident, she attributed it to the resentment she had been harboring in her body.

"I truly believe that the cancer developed and needed to be burned out of my body because I was quite literally burnt out on Fault," she said. Regardless of how it developed, at this stage in her life, Marka realized that it is much more constructive to accept where she is and ask, "What now?" than to simmer in Fault. As for who or what she is asking for guidance on this, her ability to zoom out and see the big picture of her unique life path has been aided by her spiritual beliefs.

Raised both Jewish and Christian, Marka was always perplexed by organized religion. But at around age fourteen, she discovered a Hare Krishna group and a spiritual practice in which she felt more welcomed.

"I think I stopped asking 'why me' when I connected my Body Grief to my belief in reincarnation and soul groups," she said. "I believe very strongly that we each come into this world to experience different things, and that with each new lifetime, there is something new to learn." This belief helps Marka live with more compassion, and to be accepting of whatever life brings her way, no matter how challenging. She speaks of allowing what she calls "God love" to flow through her and into her life, which she describes as a love that is unconditional, that can be trusted completely, and that she can extend toward herself and others in the form of compassion, kindness, and acceptance. And she believes in the concept of the "soul journey," or her spirit's path of self-discovery. This has also helped Marka recognize that her body is not who she is; it is just the place where she lives in this life.

Having been to the brink and back so many times in her Body Grief has given Marka confidence in her spiritual beliefs, which in turn gives her complete faith and trust that whatever she is experiencing, she is where she is supposed to be. Anytime she falls back into Fault, she is able to remind herself that, for whatever reason, her Body Grief is part of her soul's assignment in this life.

I have been the direct recipient of the wisdom that she has gained as a result. Marka has taught me so much about the spiritual nature of Body Trust, which often lies just on the other side of Fault. When people look at her they may feel pity, but she has become my muse.

Recently, somebody on social media had messaged me privately to say that I was living their "worst fear" because I just kept having "bad things happen to me." All they could see was somebody who was chronically ill and in a wheelchair with no uterus. But having Marka as a role model in my life has helped me develop a zoomed-out perspective that moves me beyond Fault.

When I look at my life, I see somebody who is on a healing path, who is managing their pain, who is cancer-free, and who is independent thanks to their mobility aids. I see someone who has learned to feel their emotions and be with their pain, and who is also able to focus on the present while planning for tomorrow with abundance and hope. I told Marka that if I "ended up like her," I would be honored. At this, her eyes softened and welled up. She smiled, her chin lifted, and I could see her inner prima ballerina come out, the person she will always be beyond the confines of her body.

If Marka's story shows us anything, it's how damn unfair the world can be. When we are in touch with this truth, finding Fault in our Body Grief is only natural. But what we do in this phase and how we cope with the emotions that arise, can help us move along within the healing process. Fault and blame can bring comfort and information, but they can also manifest in rage. Rather than let your anger consume you, I challenge you to become empowered by it, and to let it be fuel for your "What now?" even as the flames of your anger light the pathway into the next phase of Body Grief: Fight.

AFFIRMATIONS

"I am willing to keep leaning into my discomfort."

"Change and comfort cannot and do not coexist."

"Sometimes things happen for no reason."

"Right now, it is like this."

"I am allowed to take care of my needs no matter how I feel."

JOURNAL PROMPTS

What emotions arise when you solve something or "fix" something? Does that feel satisfactory to you? Why do you think that is, and where does that come from? Would you describe yourself as a "fixer"? If you were talking to a close friend about your Body Grief and how hard it has been to live with the sadness lately, how would you feel if they tried to immediately "fix it" and why?

SEVEN

Fight: At War with What Is

Me and my body had a deal. It was my deal with the devil."

My father, Ed Mattingly, had told himself a long time ago that his body would not break, no matter how hard he worked. As the owner of a house painting business, his deal with the devil of Perceived Body Betrayal served him well—until, at age sixty-two, he fell from a three-story ladder and almost died.

My father knew what was happening as soon as the ladder began to tip backward. Within a split second he was thrown into the air, somersaulting backward as his life flashed before his eyes. Luckily, his body hit the second-story roof on the way down, a bounce that sprung him fifteen feet away from the house where he had been painting the third-story shutters. Landing hard on his ribs on his well-manicured suburban lawn, he found himself gasping for air trying to find his breath. Lying there unable to move, my father thought his time was up.

Miraculously, my dad found he could stand. As he continued to gasp for breath, doing his best to ignore the crushing pain in his foot, he scanned the lawn. His ladder and painting equipment had landed a few feet away, the tin of bright white paint splashed all over the neighbor's nice brick pathway. The neighbor rushed out to help him, and he was overcome with feelings of embarrassment and shame, which drowned out the fear that coursed through his veins, as well as his relief that his life had been spared. He'd been working as a painter for over forty years. How could he have let something so stupid happen to him?

Eager to gloss over the incident as quickly as possible, my dad called his foreman to help clean up and climbed into his truck. His hands folded in his lap and head hung low, he sat in the driver's seat as the pain from the fall finally started to seep in. Looking concerned, the neighbor asked if they should call an ambulance. But my dad just shook his head and smiled. "No, that won't be necessary." He glanced at the clock on the dashboard. It was early. He still had several jobs to complete before the day was done, so he fought to collect himself, pushing through the pain in his body and the noise in his mind and onto the next thing.

Within moments of experiencing a devastating shock to his system that had in fact resulted in serious physical injury, my father found himself in Fight. It was a place he had been trained for, and which he knew well. In the back of his mind, he could hear the words he had repeated to the painters he had been training for decades: "My grandfather was on ladders until he was sixty-five. He taught me to eat lunch with my left hand and paint with my right."

On the surface, the message was that you live to work. But it meant much more than that to my dad. Everything he did was motivated by what he truly loved most: his family. This meant waking at three a.m. each day to be able to get enough work in so he could still be home in time for dinner, homework, TV time, dance recitals, and other family activities. Even now that we were all grown up, his grandfather's message ran deep in his veins. His purpose—the reason he was even here—was to provide for the ones he loved. On the day of his accident, this could all have been taken away from him. He had to keep fighting.

It was only after he had finished his workday, came home, showered, and woken my mom from her nap that my dad took a moment to acknowledge what had happened.

"I'm sorry," he said shakily, lifting his left hand, with its hard calluses and white paint covering the cracks surrounding his nail beds, to wipe away a tear, "I almost died." My mom immediately got her nurse supplies out and tended to my dad's multiple bruises, scrapes, and cuts. Her tenderness melted some of the bravado of his Fight, and yet still he refused to go to the ER. There was no time for his body to be broken, and no space to feel his Body Grief. My dad had a business to run, a family to take care of—and besides, he had made his deal with the devil.

Fight: "I'm Going to Beat This Thing"

When we're in Dismissal, we either consciously or unconsciously choose to ignore our pain and struggle. In the Shock phase of Body Grief, we almost immediately dissociate or distract ourselves from this truth. With Apology, we downplay what is happening. In Fault, we find something, often ourselves or our defective body, to blame.

No wonder that by the time we find ourselves in Fight, we are ready to just get on with it and live our lives already! And so, we muscle through and push down any pain, discomfort, and challenging emotions that may accompany our Body Grief as we do whatever it takes to carry on as normal.

Fight is our attempt to take back control and regain power over our body and our circumstances. We are the ones in charge here, we think, and no level of pain, discomfort, or inconvenience is going to be the boss of us. Fight can be seen as a sign of strength and an expression of mind over matter: "I will not let this beat me." There's no denying this can be incredibly useful, as this mindset can get us past the most painful and impossible-seeming parts of our Body Grief journey. For instance, when I was in the grips of my greatest physical pain, all I could focus on was the mess in my house. Every dust bunny that rolled past me was a reminder of the mess in my mind, so I fought back by cleaning. Cleaning is a form of distraction that I use to this day.

In other words, it is natural to want to Fight against a perceived threat to our well-being. In fact, it's part of our fight, flight, freeze, or fawn stress response, although when it comes to Body Grief, it is often our last resort. We find ourselves in Fight when there is nowhere to run to (flight/Shock), no more denying what is happening to us (freeze/Dismissal), and no bargaining our way out of this (fawn/Apology).

This is also where the good old fear of missing out (FOMO) creeps in, something I experienced as applying for disability was dangled in my face as an option following my first brain surgery. Yes, I absolutely qualified, and I could easily justify spending the following two years not working and focusing on nothing but my healing. I could have chosen to see this as a gift. But I had a business to build and all sorts of exciting opportunities ahead of me. I didn't want to miss out on any of it because, you know, YOLO! You only live once.

FOMO and YOLO often go hand in hand in keeping us in Fight. Having a YOLO attitude can make us feel rebellious and carefree in our Fight, sort of like a youthful rebel who just doesn't care. This can help flip us out of apathy and Hopelessness (the phase of the Body Grief process that we'll be discussing in the next chapter) and keep living our life to the fullest. In my case, this meant saying yes to every prospective client, continuing to grow my business, and consistently showing up on social media, even while in the depths of my Body Grief.

But as much as I care deeply about my work, and despite how passionate I am about helping people, what was really driving me to push through my pain and suffering as I attempted to keep doing it all—because YOLO—was my fear of missing out on everything I saw my counterparts experiencing and achieving. I wanted everything they were having! If I couldn't have my youth, my health, and my physical ability, I might as well have my career.

And there it was again, blaring as loud as could be: the internalized ableist belief that my worth as a human being is directly linked to my productivity, a belief that had been passed down the generations, and which was reinforced everywhere I looked.

At the end of the day, Fight might *look* strong, but it is really motivated by fear, fear that if we surrender to our Body Grief, listen to what our body needs, and take the time to heal, we will be left behind. In a world where time is money and our very survival is tied to our ability to perform, Fight helps us to armor up and go to battle against what we perceive as our defective, ailing body and its needs. But when we stay in Fight too long, this finds us knowingly, and sometimes proudly, ignoring our bodily cues, and only deepening our Body Grief.

SIGNS YOU ARE IN FIGHT

The first sign that you are in Fight is that you are overriding your bodily cues and pushing on through any pain, discomfort, and emotional dysregulation you may be experiencing in your Body Grief. This may be accompanied by physical sensations such a shortness of breath, your heart beating quickly, warmth in the body, a headache, feeling anxious, and a sense of urgency, all of which are signs that the central nervous system is on high alert. In these moments, Fight can feel almost like a manic attempt to keep it all together. You may decide you need another coffee or a stiff drink to power through. You may give yourself a stern talking to, demanding that you "stop being so pathetic."

You also know you're in Fight when you're feeling easily triggered, as if anything could set you off—every Instagram post, TV show, or well-meaning comment from a friend or family member is liable to spark either an angry diatribe or a teary-eyed tantrum. You find yourself lashing out at others who are genuinely trying to help you, as you perceive their efforts as "proof" that you are indeed weak, helpless, and pathetic in your Body Grief.

You may also be in denial about your reality, as Fight leans on Dismissal in order to justify the herculean effort of keeping calm and carrying on. In this case, Fight can look like directly disobeying doctors' orders, avoiding or side-stepping questions about how you are doing, or packing your calendar with social events. It can be overworking, pushing through pain, partaking in risk-taking behavior to "prove" how brave you are, or being the "tough" one in challenging situations. All of these are simply ways to combat the overwhelming truth: this is Body Grief.

"Everybody Loves a Fighter": How the Hero Complex Makes Us Sick

Before we look at what happens when we get stuck in Fight, let's unpack what makes this the most socially acceptable and even celebrated phase of the Body Grief process. Society loves a fighter, doesn't it? We are often praised for our ability to overcome the odds, and we admire others who exhibit strength in the face of adversity, from storybook heroes and movie protagonists to inspiring news stories and viral TikToks. This instinct is rooted in survivalism. For previous generations—going right back to our hunter-gatherer roots—an ability to triumph in the face of seemingly insurmountable obstacles and challenges was literally the difference between life and death. All of us carry this belief that we must fight for our place in the food chain, even though we live in an age where most of us, especially in a first world country like the United States, have "enough," including enough time to reflect, to feel, to heal, and to be with our Body Grief. When we forget this, it is easy to stay stuck in Fight.

Looking at our complex human history, we can see how much of our fight impulse is also rooted in cultural and economic systems of power. Within extractive capitalism, survival is connected to our ability to work, earn, and be productive, and to continue to do so until we are no longer able. Fear of our body failing us and not being able to perform according to these expectations is what fuels our Fight. Unfortunately, this model breeds perfectionism, comparison, and envy, making it a core driver of ableism, ageism, and racism. And the thing about biases is, they're designed to spread. We fear becoming disabled, which makes us discriminate against disabled people. We fear aging, which makes us dismissive of older people.

When you layer Body Grief on top of this, it becomes easy to see how some people feel like they spend their whole lives in Fight. When you and your body are already perceived as being less-than because of your race, gender, ability, or whatever else, and when this results in fewer opportunities, lower wages, and even threats to your physical well-being, survival becomes your only option. There is no time to be with your Body Grief; you have no option but to keep fighting whatever is happening in your body to keep showing up.

For those of us in lower income brackets—frequently people who are otherwise marginalized—there often *isn't* enough time to stop and give our body what it needs. I mean, how is a single mom working full time while getting her college degree supposed to even get to the doctor when she gets sick, let alone take time off to rest and prioritize her body and its needs?

As another example, the aging process is something we will all hopefully get to experience. Yet aging is often presented as something awful that happens *to* us and that we are the *victims* of, as if gray hairs, lines, and sagging skin are something we can and must fight against. Capitalist beauty standards present these signs of age as flaws, which can trigger intense Body Grief as we watch our youth slowly ebbing away. (Keep in mind that youth is a valuable commodity to capitalism, as young people are seen as being more nondisabled, and therefore more productive workers.) Here the antiaging industry, currently valued at $34 billion in the United States alone, swoops in, targeting our fear of becoming the victims of age. Elixirs, injectables, serums, and procedures: that is *a lot* of profit being generated by our fear-driven fight against the passage of time.

This fight may be marketed as empowerment and living our #bestlife. But when it comes to healing our Body Grief, our best life will always be the one where we are able to recognize which battles are worth fighting, and when it is time to accept where we are at and advocate for our body and what it needs *today*—while also recognizing the influence of any internalized isms that may be at play.

Of course, nobody wants to be seen as a victim, to be seen as weak. Sick and disabled people, people in recovery, and people who are being unfairly discriminated against have probably heard the saying "Don't be a victim of your circumstances." It's supposed to inspire us to keep fighting to overcome our challenges, to create the lives we deserve. But when the obstacles we are faced with are structural—streets without sidewalks, stores without ramps or accessible toilets, and cities without accessible public transportation—this unfairly places all the responsibility on the individual to fight back. As we've learned, there is power in the action that asking "What now?" incites. But when the obstacles we face are literally insurmountable, becoming burned out in Fight only results in fatigue and isolation.

Release the Tension

When faced with a threat, it is natural to want to grit your teeth and white-knuckle it. But if you can release this tension by quite literally unclenching your muscles and letting go of the Fight in your body, you can bring yourself back to neutral. To do this, drop your shoulders from your ears and your tongue from the roof of your mouth. Take a giant inhale followed by a long, slow exhale, the kind of exhale that embarrasses you in yoga class, the audible kind. Now do it again.

As you continue to breathe and let your tongue lie flat on the bottom of your mouth, remind yourself that this moment is all you really have, and that right now, it is like this. From this place, you can begin to be with your body, to listen, and to discern what it truly needs.

What We Resist Persists:
The Cost of Fighting Too Hard

As we have learned, the impulse to fight is deeply ingrained in many of us, and sometimes it's true that the best option is to put on a brave face and muscle through. It can also be incredibly important to stand up to the various systems of oppression that we encounter in our daily lives, and to demand something different for ourselves and others. But the longer we fight against what is happening in our body, the longer we prolong the pain and suffering we may be experiencing as a result. This is the double-edged sword of Fight.

Watching my dad fight against his Body Grief reminded me how much I am my father's daughter. The powerful work ethic and can-do attitude I inherited from him have served me well: I fought for my eating disorder recovery while working multiple jobs to make ends meet. I also got through graduate school and opened my own business, even as I was grappling with the onset of my disabilities. But the fighter in me also prevented me from accepting the help I needed in the early stages of my chronic illness, prolonging my agony and keeping me at war with my body. As the saying goes: "What we resist persists."

Four months after my initial diagnosis, I had my first brain surgery. During this time, I had continued to work on establishing my practice, as well as working as a nanny, a secretary, and a teacher's assistant, all while holding down my internship fieldwork for my graduate degree in therapy. I was determined not to let something like my health get in the way of me pursuing my dreams.

The day after I came home from the hospital, I must have looked like I was out of my mind, down on my hands and knees in my home office, heaving through the pain and feeling like I was being hit from all sides. During the surgery, two stents were placed in the back of my head to save my eyesight, and they felt like heavy magnets sitting in the paper-thin veins at the base of my brain. My body also hadn't taken to the surgery just yet, and I was experiencing significant high pressure in my spine and brain. My head felt as if it was about to pop off my hot-rod spine, and my lower back was spasming out of control. When my shaking hand grazed my brand-new pink lace undies, I discovered they were covered in blood. Fuck, I'd gotten my period, too! The pain was becoming intolerable, but I was done with being a victim, and I had work to do. So I got up off the ground, wiped my tears away, changed my clothes and inserted a tampon, and put on a pad the size of a diaper. Then I took a deep breath, applied some lip gloss, and signed on to my next Zoom meeting.

My doctors had prescribed pain medication for this exact circumstance, but I was determined not to become dependent on anything outside of me to function. Taking the pain meds would be giving in. Both Sean and my father had tried to convince me to pause my practice and sign on for disability payments while I took time off to recover. But I saw this, too, as a cop-out. I brushed them off, telling them, "It's not a big deal! I have to make money! I'm doing important work, and my clients need me!" I was desperate not to let my disability beat me. Like all of us, I had been taught that my worth lay in my ability to be a productive member of society. But the more I fought against my new reality, the more pain and suffering I ended up experiencing.

My unwillingness to admit defeat was also saturated in internalized ableism, something that was brought home yet again by my refusal to accept that I needed to be in a wheelchair. It took three terrifying falls in my house, two of which landed me back in the hospital— once in emergency surgery—for me to accept that I was no longer able to get around safely by myself. This reality was so hard to accept.

I could get along just fine with a walker or rollator, couldn't I? Transitioning to a wheelchair felt like a demotion and sign that I was getting "worse." Because of this, I fought tooth and nail against accepting help and allowing myself access to tools that would make my life significantly easier.

This is how getting stuck in Fight can become maladaptive. Not only did this attitude create unnecessary suffering, but it also resulted in another serious injury to my spine. Simply put, fighting my need for pain meds, fighting to stay employed versus signing on for disability, and fighting my need for a wheelchair were hurting me both literally and figuratively. The reality is, all of these forms of aid are simply tools, ones representing amazing medical and social advances, that are available to help people live with more comfort and ease in their Body Grief. It is due to our own internalized ableism, healthism, and capitalism, all of which are so deeply stigmatized and misunderstood, that we would often rather stay in Fight than succumb to said isms.

For example, despite my doctors assuring me that it was safe to use my pain medication as prescribed, I was still terrified that I would end up a statistic in the opioid crisis. The risk of addiction is very real with this kind of medication, and yet I also knew that I needed it. I also knew that my fears were being stoked by visions of being labeled as "weak" for using pain meds, or ending up an "addict," just like in those awful movies and TV specials. These are supposedly cautionary tales—but the sensationalist nature of reporting on the opioid crisis also helps to demonize mental illness and addiction. Part of me knew this, but I couldn't help it: I was terrified!

It was the same when I sat in my new wheelchair for the first time at my physical therapist's office. Using it would officially make me a "disabled person." This was another ableist thought: I know very well that disabilities come in all shapes and sizes, and that disability can be both visible and invisible. But my fear that this was my new reality was real. I looked my PT directly in the eyes. She knew the full extent of my medical history, and I asked her outright, "Do you really believe I need this?"

She smiled kindly and just said, "Jayne, look at you." I glanced over at the mirror where I had watched myself do exercises to strengthen my spine. Taking in my neck brace, my pelvic brace, my service dog on one side, and my rollator on the other, all I could see was misery and pain. God. My body was working so hard on my behalf. Why was I fighting this tool that would simply allow it to function with more ease? But because Fight was what came naturally to me, because Fight was strong and Fight was what worked—at least, according to my inner ableist narrative—it was hard to accept my reality.

It's easy to see when somebody else is only hurting themselves by staying stuck in Fight—especially somebody you love, like my mom with my dad—but it is so much harder to accept this in yourself. Having needs makes us vulnerable.

Looking back, part of me wonders how my story would have gone had I quit fighting my illness and accepted the help and tools I needed earlier in my Body Grief journey. Chances are, had I taken a couple of years off work to rest and heal, I would not have needed so many surgeries. But then, I might also have not gotten to where I am today, writing this book and sharing what I have learned about the Body Grief process with you. (And can you see what's happening here? This is me going backward from Fight into Fault, as I turn the blame for my suffering back onto myself.)

Ultimately, the key to working through Fight is to recognize when it is helping us live more fully and when it is just going to wear us out. Yes, the fighter in me likely prolonged my pain, and even made it worse. But she is also part of who I am. Fighting for my purpose, my joy, and my work also helped motivate and energize me when I was at my lowest point. Untangling our ableist belief that vulnerability is weakness is how we move forward. To get the help we need, we must first accept that it is okay to be weak.

When I was finally able to quit fighting my illness and reach for the tools that were available to me, I discovered that they brought me the exact freedom, relief, and ease that I had been fighting against my body for.

Exercise:

A PLANNED REBELLION

It is healthy for our inner child, especially our inner teenager, to want to rebel now and again—to fight against the system. Fight can serve this purpose within the Body Grief process, which in turn can feel incredibly liberating. When used as an adaptive coping tool, a Planned Rebellion is a way to lean into our Fight in a healthy way because it can help us scratch the Fight "itch," if you will, without doing us any harm.

The key to planning a moment of rebellion is to discern if this Fight is worth fighting for. Ask yourself: What will I get out of this, and what will it take out of me? One way to know if a Planned Rebellion is adaptive is how you feel afterward: Are you feeling fulfilled on some level, or has it left you feeling depleted?

Here are two examples from my life:

1. I decided to go out for margaritas and pedicures this weekend. I understood that my body would be sore, and that the excursion would take a lot of energy. But I was feeling isolated, lonely, and in need of girl time and

laughter; in other words, I had cabin fever. I knew that spending time with my girlfriends would fill my social and emotional cup.

2. Since my spine is fused, I can no longer twerk. As a former dancer, this is devastating to me! I have therefore made it my life's purpose to find a way to shake my ass working *with* my mobility aids. Instead of pushing myself to twerk like I used to, I will take my rollator, Pearl, make sure her brakes are on (because safety first), turn up my speakers, and let loose, experimenting with how my body can move now.

3. At first, I felt silly, as if someone was judging me. There I was, leaning on the arms of my walker trying to throw ass like I was twenty-five and nondisabled. But I just tell myself, "Right now, it's like this." I lean into it and rebel against my internalized ableism. I feel completely liberated after one of my twerking sessions with Pearl, almost as if I am getting to know a new part of me. This feeling of liberation lets me know that I am rebelling in a healthy way against my Body Grief.

"I Am Only Human": Moving through Fight Means Choosing Your Battles

As we have seen time and again, our ability to be with our Body Grief, in whatever phase of the process we are cycling through, often lies in our ability to accept where our body is at. This is especially true when we get stuck in Fight. And in this case, acceptance lies in learning when to keep fighting, and when to let it go.

DISMANTLE YOUR UNICORN COMPLEX

First and foremost, acceptance means recognizing that you are only human, and that living in a body means experiencing some degree of pain, loss, and suffering. Of course, more often than not, we believe the opposite. I call this the "unicorn complex," or the belief that you are the exception to the rule. Society often praises and even subtly encourages this—if everybody loves a fighter, we love stories of miraculous recoveries even more!

When we are in Fight, our unicorn complex is often lurking in the shadows. It can manifest in thoughts such as *I am stronger than other people, I will be able to fight this thing*, and *The rules do not apply to me.* Or it can look like a manic attempt to override what is happening in our body and get on with our life. For me, this meant taking clients the day after my first brain surgery, not taking my pain meds, and refusing my mobility aids. For my dad, it lay in the belief that his body would not break, no matter how hard he worked. For somebody fighting against growing old, it may look like continuing to splurge hundreds, even thousands, of dollars on sparkly antiaging products and procedures, even when they deliver questionable results.

A unicorn complex is particularly prevalent in circumstances where we perceive the drivers of our Body Grief as somehow being reversible when they're not, as is the case with most autoimmune conditions, chronic illnesses, cancer diagnoses, loss of mobility, skin conditions, insomnia, hair loss, and, again, the aging process. If we can just fight hard enough, we think, we can crack the magic code, turn back time, and become happy and healthy again.

Of course, this is magical thinking. Fight becomes another form of self-preservation: we desperately *want* to believe we are in control of our body and its functions, because we want to believe we can get "better." The alternative is that we have very little control over any of this, and that life is anything but fair.

Here's the truth: we are not unicorns. We are human beings whose bodies break, get sick, and "fail us" every day. When we fight this, know that we do so out of our fear of only being human. One powerful way to undo this mindset is to lean into big and small moments of gratitude. Expressing gratitude, even when we are suffering, can be incredibly humbling and grounding. "I am grateful I woke up today." "I am grateful for clean water." "I am grateful that my pain is less today."

GIVE UP THE FIGHT

It might *look* like we're in control, but when we're in the grips of a unicorn complex, the amygdala is online and we are in the fight part of the fight, flight, freeze, or fawn response. In my dad's case, this looked like getting into his car and heading to another job minutes after he fell off a three-story ladder. It wasn't until one a.m. the night of his fall that Ed finally accepted he is only human, gave up the fight, and agreed to go to the hospital, which turned out to be healing on many levels for him. Let me show you how his story played out.

It took an impassioned call from me—the daughter who has dedicated her life to helping people acknowledge their Body Grief—to get him there. My mom and my sisters had both pleaded with him to get himself checked out. When my mom called me, I made her put me on speakerphone and told my dad that I would get on the next flight out if he didn't go to the ER to get a comprehensive exam. This was my Momma Bear coming out, and it was exactly the same tactic my mom had used with me when the ER doctor who gave me my initial spinal tap refused to take my symptoms seriously.

I stood my ground, but so did my dad. He even yelled, "No! I won't go, no!" I was stunned. My dad never yells at us, ever. How could the same person who had advocated so strongly for me to take care of myself following my surgery be so negligent of his own health? And then it clicked: he thought he was the exception to the rule. He was in Fight, and he had a bad case of the unicorn complex. And damn was this indeed complex in Ed's case.

Fight is a very comfortable state to be in for people like my dad. As a cisgender, heterosexual American male, Ed may embody the ideal normal. But he is *also* impacted by internalized patriarchy, capitalism, and ableism, consolidating in the deeply entrenched belief that "I am only worthy if I can provide." Of course, many queer, non-white people of all genders can relate to this. But the message that we only have value if we are able to work, make money, push our feelings aside, and produce is especially potent for men who have been told that their whole purpose is to provide for a wife and kids. This is all part of what keeps the system well oiled, and it leaves very little space for feelings and Body Grief.

Feeling all of this on my dad's behalf, I started to cry silently; but still, I wouldn't give up. I was going to fight for him to get the help he needed. My mom took me off speaker and said, "We'll call you when we get there."

To this day, I don't know what happened then on the other end of the line, but twenty minutes later my mom called back to tell me that my dad was being triaged in the ER. The doctors couldn't believe he'd survived the fall. It wasn't just cuts and bruises; he was diagnosed with broken ribs and a fractured ankle, and sent for PT, mental health counseling, and rest. It was just the beginning of a long healing journey that is still ongoing.

My dad still can't articulate why it took him so long to get help, but I have no doubt it was because he was deeply locked in Fight—and had been for much of his life. In a way, his accident was a blessing in disguise. It made him finally accept that he is only human, with human feelings and weaknesses like the rest of us. His whole life he had been taught to "man up" and that to be vulnerable was to be weak. Finally quitting fighting against his body and its needs was humbling for him, in a good way.

In the weeks and months following the incident, I witnessed him choose rest, go to counseling, and accept help for the first time in his life. He has become his daughter's father.

Giving up the fight often looks like finding more ease and taking the path of less resistance. This may also be where we must face our internalized isms as they will likely rear their head. For instance, if your Body Grief involves an injury, disability, or chronic illness, your mobility may have been affected. Because both ableism and ageism dictate that only mobile bodies are valid, it is common to fight the need for help in this instance. But giving up the fight and investing in a shower chair and a raised toilet seat may be incredibly helpful, and offer so much in terms of safety, comfort, and independence. It is stigma that keeps us from accessing what we need. Trust me, I have been there. And damn, does it feel good when we challenge our internalized isms and stop fighting what we need.

ADDRESS YOUR ENVY

It is natural to compare our bodies, achievements, and lives to others. Social media in particular capitalizes on this trait, which in turn stems from what the various isms tell us about which types of bodies are more deserving, aka the ideal normal. But the reality is, there will always be somebody who seems like they have it better than us, whose body never fails or betrays them, and who is living an enviably charmed life. Enter envy: another core driver of Fight that prevents us from being and working with our Body Grief.

Envy can even be very motivating, as it can help show us what we want and give us the energy to fight for it. After all, if they get to have it all, why can't we? But when our Fight is driven by envy, we become resentful of those we perceive as having "perfect" or even just "normal" bodies. This is also where FOMO creeps back in. Our fear of missing out and being left behind means now we will do whatever we can to prove we are as good and as deserving as them.

Envy can sound like:

"I wish my problems were as simple as theirs."

"They don't know how good they have it."

"If only that were my life."

All of this is very normal—and it can keep us stuck in Fight long past the point of being constructive. To address your envy, start by identifying the thought at the root of it, then use CBT to reframe this thought, alter your perspective, and choose a different behavior. For example, say your friend has been posting bikini pics on Instagram. As much as you love and appreciate them, this has triggered envy in you, leading you to fight your natural body shape and size with various extreme diets. At the root of your envy is fatphobia, which tells us only small bodies are attractive and worthy of being loved. From this place, you might start filling your social feeds with examples of people celebrating their bodies at all different sizes, helping you decolonize your own internalized fatphobia and begin to lean back into Body Trust.

EMBRACE THE JOY OF MISSING OUT

As we've learned, Fight is often our last (and socially acceptable) resort when we feel backed into a corner by our Body Grief. On the surface, it may look like we are coming out on top, but as both my dad's story and the example above show, the real healing work, as always, lies in accepting the body we are in today just as it is, and giving *this* body what it needs. This means embracing JOMO: the joy of missing out.

On the surface, JOMO sounds like it will make our life smaller, but it's actually about being more discerning regarding where we place our energy. Instead of trying to "have it all"—or even just having what that one particular influencer we are particularly obsessed with appears to be having—getting really clear on what we truly want, what our unique body needs, and our true capacity to enjoy it to the fullest is the key to moving through this phase of Body Grief.

For me, embracing the joy of missing out meant realizing I didn't have to say yes to everything. It was okay to build my business much more slowly, because my well-being was more important to me than fighting to squeeze every single moment out of each and every day.

For you, JOMO might look like being much more selective about what you spend your precise energy on. In your daily life, it might mean saying no to events, trips, and gatherings that are not accessible, as this may flip you into Apology and Fault, draining your energy and causing you to hurt yourself, feel worse, and miss out on things that are accessible to you. It might mean going for a leisurely stroll and coffee with a friend rather than day drinking, as a way of protecting your mental health.

In whatever ways you find your joy of missing out, instead of fighting against your body, you will learn to listen deeply to its signals and its whispers, and to give it what it needs at any given moment.

Reflection

What are some of the things you have had to accept missing out on as the result of being with your Body Grief? In what ways, if any, did you try to fight this and push through? What messages did you receive from others and from society about what it means to "keep fighting" and to "not let this thing beat you"? How did this make you feel?

To help you go from FOMO to JOMO, take a moment to reflect on your values and your needs today, rather than your desires. For example, if you are envious of someone being able to go for a run, sit with this envy and ask what is underneath this desire. Perhaps this is simply the need to move your body and feel energized. What are some other ways you could give this to yourself?

"It Is What It Is": Meg's Story

Some of the most powerful examples of acceptance as an antidote to Fight can be found among those living with invisible illnesses. Conditions like fibromyalgia, multiple sclerosis, Lyme disease, and chronic fatigue syndrome are routinely dismissed by medical professionals while quietly robbing individuals of their agency, their ability, and their lives. It is a fight just to be seen and believed, something Meg experienced during the three years after she was diagnosed with long COVID.

Meg couldn't believe she had been living in this heavy haze day in and day out since getting COVID in the fall of 2020. A migraine was coming on, and she reached for her cane as the kids got ready for school, thinking back to that scary morning when she first tested positive for COVID. She had been so sick; she wasn't sure if she was going to make it. While the most acute symptoms had since passed, the severe fatigue had stayed with her ever since. Meg could sleep twelve or thirteen hours a day and still feel so tired, it was as if she had a hundred-pound weight hanging off her body. She had also developed an autonomic dysfunction called postural orthostatic tachycardia syndrome (POTS) that caused her to faint on a regular basis. Her husband and kids were constantly finding her on the floor, sometimes with a head wound. To top it off, her migraines had gotten worse, as had her anxiety, and she lived with chronic pain that sometimes felt unbearable.

Meg had seen countless doctors and specialists, none of whom had been able to tell her what was wrong with her—but all who promised Meg that she would start to feel better soon, and that her life and body would eventually go back to normal. But that hadn't happened yet, and she was so over it. This wasn't the life she'd signed up for. Meg had two young children, a husband, a career as a dog trainer, and a life to live on the Tennessee mountains. It all seemed so unfair, and her fear that she would never get better had her constantly in Fight.

The previous October, her kids had been invited to a Halloween party. "And I said, screw it!" recalled Meg. "I'm taking my cane, I'm taking my meds, I'm taking this awful migraine, and I'm taking my kids to that party. I will be a shell of my former self, but I will be there! Fuck it. I don't care if I'm only going to feel worse, because YOLO!"

Meg was determined not to let her illness steal this precious time with her family. But instead of creating a happy memory with her kids, the shooting pain in her head and the aura from her migraine made her feel like she was dying, and she spent the party counting the minutes until she could go lie down.

Over the years, Meg lost count of the number of times doctors had turned her away, passed her along, given her empty promises, or prescribed grandiose treatment plans that were not covered by her insurance, only for her symptoms to show no improvement (all serving to keep her in Dismissal). There is still so little research on long COVID, making it incredibly challenging to navigate as a patient. And so for a long time, feeling like she was all alone in her Body Grief, all Meg could do was keep fighting. This got her through some murky waters, but after three years she felt the fight beginning to ebb out of her. Meg was exhausted. Perhaps she would finally have to accept that this was her new normal and begin to adapt her life to fit her and her body's changing needs, instead of the other way around.

So one day, Meg canceled yet another exploratory appointment with a new specialist, rescheduling it for a few months down the line. If she was still in Fight, she would have pushed herself to keep it. But once she accepted her reality, she knew that the appointment was likely to only deplete her further physically, emotionally, and financially. Leaning into JOMO in this instance brought a sense of relief, even if her symptoms remained the same. She would keep on fighting, but on her body's schedule and on her own terms.

"It is what it is"—these five simple words of acceptance have become Meg's guiding light, helping her discern in each moment what is worth fighting for, whether it's more time to rest when she needs it, or the peace of mind that comes from not needing all the answers. She describes acceptance as a constant thread in the tapestry of her healing. One moment she will be in a dark, downward spiral, staring at her wheelchair thinking, *How is this my life?* And then she will take a deep breath, move into the seat of the chair, and simply enjoy the freedom that it brings her.

If you take anything away from Meg's story, and from what we have learned about Fight in this chapter, it is this: sometimes it is okay to give up the fight and let life be smaller if it means we are able to find moments of peace and happiness with the body we are in today. Sometimes it is okay to *not* do the hard thing, to *not* push your body to the max, and to accept that rest really is the best answer. Yes, leaning into Fight can mean learning how to advocate and say no on behalf of your body. But it is okay to lean right back out and give up the fight at any time during the Body Grief process. After all, continuing to fight what feels like a losing battle against our body, against our needs, and against the cruel and unjust systems of oppression, can lead to us feeling utterly without hope—which is the next phase of Body Grief, Hopelessness.

AFFIRMATIONS

"I am not perfect."

"Perfection is not realistic."

"It is normal to compare myself to others—
but I do not have to be them."

"I am worthy exactly as I am."

"I do not have to fight this."

JOURNAL PROMPTS

Play the script forward. If you quit fighting against what you
are experiencing, what would happen? What would be the
worst-case scenario? How would you survive it? What would
come next? Spend a few minutes free writing, imagining all
the possibilities.

EIGHT

Hopelessness/Hope: There Is a Way Forward

Kate hit yet another rock bottom in her Body Grief journey after she was diagnosed with treatment-resistant depression. Sitting in her psychiatrist's office, everything went blurry as her doctor's words echoed in her brain, and Shock caused her to dissociate from her surroundings. She took a deep breath and shook her hands, using the tools she had learned throughout years of depression to ground herself and bring her back into the room. At this point, she had been living with her depression for over a decade, trying various medications, treatments, and interventions. Nothing had worked.

"You have two options left," her doctor told her. "Electroconvulsive therapy, also known as shock therapy, or deep brain stimulation, which involves brain surgery."

At that moment, Kate was transported back to the fall of 2012. A bottle of pills shook in her hands. She was terrified, and taking her own life had seemed like the only answer that made sense to her brain at the time. The therapy she had been offered for her depression when it first began to take hold wasn't working, and she felt completely and utterly hopeless. The darkness she had lived with for years on end seemed to have no end. In her state of hopelessness, she decided it was enough. And so, she swallowed all the pills she had on hand and put herself to bed.

But another part of her was not ready to die. Kate eventually got up, knocked on her sister's bedroom door, and told her what she'd done. Her sister immediately woke their parents, and Kate was rushed to the nearest hospital, where she was taken care of and referred to an inpatient treatment center for depression, PTSD, and an eating disorder. It was only at this point that she finally experienced a glimmer of hope within her Body Grief journey: she had hit rock bottom, and the only way was up.

At the time, this hope led Kate to try a plethora of ways to "get better," the latest being ketamine therapy. She allowed herself to get her hopes up, as she had been promised that this would eliminate her ongoing suicidal ideations. And for a while, it was true. During her weekly ketamine infusions, thoughts of ending her life went away completely. But they came back once she stopped the routine treatments, and Kate was left with paralyzing headaches, layering on yet more Body Grief as the physical pain limited her ability to get around. After weighing the risks and benefits of staying on ketamine, her doctor was now presenting the two remaining options for treatment-resistant depression—a diagnosis that Kate was still trying to digest.

The diagnosis alone triggered yet more Body Grief for Kate. Had she gotten this prognosis earlier, she could have avoided going on and off the various medications she had been prescribed over the years and not had to suffer the grueling side effects, some of which still persisted: pain, heart palpitations, rapid weight gain, night sweats, a decrease in appetite, irritability, *increased* suicidal ideation, nausea, difficulty sleeping, fatigue . . . the list went on and on. And now, to know that the pills were never going to fix her anyway?

Once more, Kate felt the same depths of darkness that had crept over her when she had swallowed those pills. It all felt like too much to take in. She was furious with herself for getting her hopes up that the ketamine would work. How could she have been so stupid to have been duped by hope again? Kate had tried and failed so many times to fight her depression. At that moment, there was no hope, only despair and hopelessness. She felt she was destined for a life that would always be clouded by depression—despite what her doctor was telling her about these two not-so-lovely final options.

Hopelessness and Hope:
Two Sides of the Same Coin

In this story, we meet Kate at a rock-bottom moment in her Body Grief journey. Very much depleted, she has no more gas in her tank, having summoned what felt like her last reserves of strength in order to embrace the possibility that the ketamine treatments would fix her once and for all. She'd begun these infusions in full Fight—which, as we saw in the last chapter, is the most celebrated and socially accepted phase of Body Grief. But when they didn't work and all the fight left her, Kate entered the Hopelessness phase of Body Grief.

Hopelessness hits when it feels like there is no way out of our Body Grief. It can be very scary to arrive here, as it is often a dark and isolating place, filled with despair. You have probably felt Hopelessness lurking in the shadows of every story in this book, because whatever the causes of our Body Grief, there may come a time when it feels like all is lost. We have been in pain for too freaking long, we don't see things getting better, and we are hit with the realization that there is no going back to how things were. At this point, our body and our psyche begin to prepare us for the end by bringing up thoughts such as *What is the point of all of this?* or even *What is the point of living?* But anybody who has spent time in Hopelessness will know that in the moment, contemplating putting an end to our suffering and despair can actually feel calming and rational and bring a sense of relief. This is because the human mind and body are not designed to endure pain and discomfort *without proper coping skills* for too long.

Feeling hopeless in our Body Grief can be devastating, but it is also very natural. Humans are inherent problem solvers, and feeling like there is no way out goes against our very nature. At this point, giving up becomes another form of self-preservation: our psyche believes we are wasting time and energy continuing to fight the inevitable. And while this is a form of surrender, it is *not* in a way that brings relief.

When we are hopeless, it feels like being forgotten, as if the pages of life are being turned and we are being left behind forever. But while our brain tells us, "Everything is lost, it's time to give up," our *soul* knows that there is always hope. Hope that things will get better always lies right on the other side of a hopeless rock bottom. This is why Hopelessness and Hope go hand in hand. One cannot exist without the other. Just as each Body Grief story has its hopeless moment, it has its glimmers of hope, too, and with faith, proper support, and a willingness to accept our body and our situation exactly as it is, we can learn to lean into Hope when we're in this phase.

In many ways, hope is the glue that holds the Body Grief process together. Without it, we run out of gas and reach the bottom before we ever get to the good part: an expanded capacity to be in Body Trust. Hope is what revives us and gives us the energy to pull ourselves back from rock bottom. Every time we run out of steam, lose faith, or stop believing in the process, hope pushes us to take another step forward.

Hope also has a way of finding us in small, unexpected moments and ways. For example, it wasn't until Kate sat with me talking about how hopeless she felt after the ketamine treatments failed that something clicked for her.

"The ketamine helped my brain finally be able to decipher between what is a 'depressive' thought and what is a 'me' thought," she realized. "I can now identify that my suicidal ideation is my depression and not me." She paused for a second, held her coffee, and looked at me wide-eyed. "Wait, maybe ketamine treatment helped a little bit after all!"

And there it was: a tiny glimmer of Hope. It wasn't much, but it was something for Kate to hold on to as she continued to navigate her Body Grief.

SIGNS YOU ARE IN HOPELESSNESS

Hopelessness can be physically, mentally, and emotionally debilitating. You might literally feel like you have no energy left, and may find yourself feeling super lethargic, sleeping more, and clearing your calendar of activities that just feel like they will be too much. This in turn can lead to isolation, as socializing or reaching out to others literally feels like it will take more energy than you have to spare, which can then become a vicious cycle. Being alone with our thoughts when we are feeling hopeless can make us feel even more trapped, as if there is no way out of our suffering. For this reason, another sign of

Hopelessness is when we stop engaging with the things we have learned can help us feel better.

But as you will see throughout this chapter, it only takes a moment for a glimmer of Hope to burst this bubble of despair. Hope could look like putting on a nice outfit and makeup after days, even weeks, spent in your PJs. It might nudge you to reach out to a friend and suggest a coffee or FaceTime date.

When Hope is on the horizon, it feels like that exhilarating stretch you take after getting out of the car for the first time on a long drive. The air had begun to feel so stale that your body was getting used to the aches and the pains, and the minutes had begun to feel like hours. And now you have finally arrived at a rest stop. Even if it only brings a moment's respite, Hope arrives with the reminder that things can get better, even if we still need to get back into the car to keep driving to our destination.

Reflection

In the Hopelessness phase of our Body Grief journey, it is easy—*and very normal*—for depression and despair to creep in. Keeping this in mind, reflect on the experiences that have brought you to this place. What do you find yourself thinking when you are in your deepest and darkest moments in your Body Grief? And how does it feel in your body when you are feeling hopeless? Journal on this if you like and try to be as descriptive as possible. This will help you to stay objective the next time you are feeling hopeless.

Now take a deep breath and repeat this exercise, this time reflecting on the moments when you have felt a glimmer of Hope in the dark. What experiences and situations have sparked Hope on your Body Grief journey? What does it feel like to move from hopeless to hopeful? Hold on to this feeling in your body right now. Remind yourself that you can tap into this feeling, even in your darkest moments

Faith: The Gift of Desperation

When we reach a place where we feel totally hopeless, the only way is up, even if, in the moment, this can feel impossible. As my neurosurgeon once said to me, "Hope is free. Your prescription is to take three pills of hope a day!" As silly as it sounded at the time, he was telling me that having *blind faith* that things could get better could be healing in and of itself.

Now, telling somebody to have faith when they are in a deep hole of pain and suffering, and to follow this advice blindly, may seem laughable, if not downright cruel. I have been there, and I will be there again—that's how Body Grief works. But it has been by leaning into the idea that things could *possibly* get better that I have slowly crawled out of that dark hole of Hopelessness time and again, and I encourage you to try it as well. The trick is to take it "one bite at a time, like an apple," as Marka often says to me.

Looking back, my doctor's prescription of blind faith was actually a permission slip to allow things to get better—or to at least have faith that they could. At that time, I was jumping to all sorts of conclusions about what my future held based on my current reality, which left me feeling utterly hopeless. All I could see was more pain, more hospital stays, a continuing decline in my mobility, and more freedoms taken away from me by the minute. I couldn't bear another hit, and it was impossible not to spiral into Hopelessness. But now my surgeon was literally telling me that holding on to hope and having blind faith that things would get better was exactly what would allow new opportunities for healing to arise. To practice blind faith, there are two things you need to be aware of: this is not about chasing a cure, and change is inevitable.

IT IS NOT ABOUT CHASING A CURE

In my case, having blind faith helped me claw my way out of catastrophizing and investigate the nature of my pain and specific symptoms more deeply. This, in turn, led me to start working with my physical therapist, who assessed my upper body and truly listened to me. She realized that the lingering neck pain I was experiencing after my hardware removal, which I had attributed to past neck fusion surgeries, wasn't actually a structural problem in my neck at all. It was a multidirectional shoulder dislocation resulting from my EDS, which I was working with a new specialist on how to treat. This shoulder dislocation will require surgical interventions and the process of Body Grief will begin yet again—but this time, I am approaching it with a mindset of Hope.

There I'd been, preparing myself to live with this new form of pain forever, when all I had to do was allow myself to believe that things could get better and to take my next steps from this place. To have faith. It is in cases like this that a diagnosis alone will be the glimmer of Hope that we need.

The lesson here is not to chase a cure, or to expect to ever be fully free from pain. I know I will forever have this hardware in my body, *and* I have now allowed my brain to invite Hope and open itself to new options. Your pain is allowed to shift and change, your body is allowed to adapt, the world of medicine is allowed to grow, and you are allowed to get better. You are allowed to vacillate between Hopelessness and Hope. There is room for both. The Hope side of this coin is simply about allowing for space. It is not a state of mind to aim for, but a shift in perspective that allows us to trust the present enough to want to stick around for what the future holds.

CHANGE IS INEVITABLE

Central to having blind faith is the realization that while there may be no fix for our Body Grief, and although we often have no control over the process, the way in which we experience our body and whatever it is going through will always change.

You've probably heard the saying "This, too, shall pass." A popular mantra in the recovery community, it is synonymous with the nature of blind faith. Hope is the spark that exists within each of us that is willing to place our trust in the great unknown. But, as you've probably felt, humans are *not* good with the unknown, which is what makes the concept of faith scary as hell—literally! None of us truly knows what happens to us when we die, and the religious ideas of heaven and hell tap into this fear. If we just keep showing up and doing our best, day after day, then we can at least hope to find our path into the afterlife paved with rainbows.

Of course, religion has often been used to control human behavior, telling us that if we sin, then we are destined for the fires of hell. But still, faith and Hope go hand in hand. Faith that things will change begets Hope that we will get what we need to feel supported in our Body Grief. This is how both faith and Hope help us stay connected to the bigger picture and give us the strength to endure whatever we are experiencing.

Exercise:

GET TO KNOW FUTURE YOU

One way to cultivate Hope in the midst of Hopelessness is to imagine your Future You. This could be you in five days' time, one month, six months, a year, or more. Have a conversation with your Future You with the following questions and prompts.

1. What have you been feeling excited about recently?

2. What does a typical "self-care/fun" day look like to you?

3. What are your current fears?

4. What new things have you been experimenting with?

5. What has been bringing you a sense of contentment?

6. What brings you joy?

7. Do you feel supported right now?

8. What would you like to work on?

9. Tell me something I don't know about you yet.

From Hopelessness to Hope: Finding Your Reasons to Stay Alive

Let's pause here for a second and take a deep breath. Hopelessness is a heavy topic, and in many ways, it represents the lowest point of the Body Grief process. As you read on, I want to remind you that I am right here with you, and so is your breath. You also have all the other tools I've shared with you to lean on whenever a painful emotion arises, including doing a body scan, practicing Body Residency, mindful breathing, and watching your emotions like the weather. This is your gentle reminder to use them! All of that said, I want to share a particularly hopeless moment in my Body Grief journey, which also became an important turning point for me.

It was after my seventeenth time going under the knife that my surgeon told me they had failed to remove all the metal from my brain and spine. I learned this right as I was coming out of anesthesia. My eyes were swollen shut, and a beeping sound pierced my ears as my throat started to contract and cough up the intubation tube from the surgery. This was a second attempt at my final hardware removal. My body had rejected the hardware that had been placed in my neck and spine to correct for atlantoaxial instability, craniocervical instability, disc degeneration, and spinal stenosis that were part of my Ehlers-Danlos Syndrome. In a valiant attempt to protect my body from itself, my immune system was attacking not only the hardware but also my muscles and joints. Lying there in the OR, swollen and in pain, I was desperate to know if the surgery had been successful.

As I came to, my surgeon confirmed my worst fear: the hardware that remained was embedded in my spine, and if they went any deeper to remove it, I would be paralyzed from the shoulders down. The alternative—unremitting pain, inflammation, being on strong immune suppressants for life, biweekly immunotherapy infusions, continued reliance on mobility aids, and so much fucking Body Grief—was the *better option*.

For months, I had been counseled on what to expect if the hardware could not be completely removed and all along told to have hope. But in that moment, all I could do was cry; I was truly devastated. It felt as if my life was over. *How could I hold hope in this space?*, I asked myself.

As I lay there drooling, fighting the nausea from the anesthesia, I could feel the gash on the right side of my neck, right above my clavicle, covered in gauze, as well as the wound from last month's surgery sewed up like a zipper on the back of my skull. I thought about all the trauma and grief my body had experienced these past four years. *If this is it, then I want out*, I thought. I had endured sixteen surgeries and procedures at that point in time, and for what? To be stuck with hardware in my brain and spine that my body would continue to try to reject? It was utterly devastating, and I felt trapped in my body and in my Body Grief. A paraphrased lyric from Taylor Swift's album *Evermore* crossed my mind: "I wasn't be sure this pain would be forevermore." Tears stung my eyes and began to make their way slowly down my face.

But as I attempted to open my swollen eyes, I heard my dog Wheatie's collar clinking as he came around the corner, and there was Sean, my husband. He had been there with me through it all, every 911 emergency, ambulance ride, near-death experience, and heartbreaking moment of despair. On the verge of panic, I patted the blankets on the hospital bed to feel for his hand. When I started crying again, he calmed me by kissing my head and whispering in my ear, "It's going to be okay. You're okay, Bella." I could feel Wheatie's cool damp nose rest on Sean and my thumbs as we held each other's hands tightly.

I knew he was right: I was safe. And yet this was the moment, I also knew there was no going back, and that I would never fully "recover." In fact, further decline was inevitable, and I would have to say goodbye to the woman I was once and for all. I have never felt more hopeless. But the presence of my husband and my dog also brought a sense of hope, and the key to my survival in the days, weeks, and months to come would be to find my anchors: the things that keep me tethered to this world, and that literally gave me reasons to stay alive.

IDENTIFY YOUR ANCHORS

As we've learned, humans are not conditioned to be in pain for long periods of time. When we find ourselves in Hopelessness, we will immediately look for a way out, but staying with our pain is key to finding Hope. In this phase, it is therefore crucial to remind ourselves of the people, places, and things that give our lives meaning: our anchors. These special connections are what tether us to this world, no matter how hopeless things get.

My primary anchors are my relationships with my husband, my pets, and my family and friends. For example, when Sean and I started our relationship, we were an non-disabled couple, but we embarked on our marriage as an inter-abled couple. Instead of a honeymoon, I had spinal cord surgery and Sean was thrust into a week's worth of worry and secondary Body Grief. As my partner, he, too, has carried the loss of what I used to be, of the unit we had planned to become. Through it all, Sean has also been grieving. To say that he was an anchor for me during this time is the understatement of the century. His courage gave me Hope in ways that I am still learning to comprehend.

In the days after my surgery, Wheatie became my pillow and a furry tissue for my tears, and the friends who stopped by with cookies and gossip became my lifeline. (It's remarkable how a bougie bakery cookie and slice of a bestie's dating drama can bring one back down to earth.) Because I know how vital my people are to giving me hope when I am feeling hopeless, I have made these relationships a priority. I schedule daily and weekly phone calls and FaceTimes with family and friends, and virtual game nights and lunches with faraway family. I make sure Sean and I have at least one person over for dinner every week, and I visit our neighborhood friends on our golf cart every few days. I nurture my friendships as if they are sacred—and this includes regular couples therapy with Sean, which has been essential for making space for my disability and illnesses in our marriage.

In chapter 5, we learned about the importance of people outside of our immediate friends and family who share similar experiences in carrying us through our Body Grief—whether that's through group therapy, recovery programs, or grief circles. These groups can serve as powerful anchors when we are experiencing Hopelessness. The value of connecting with others who have walked this path, of hearing their stories of being in both Hopelessness and Hope, cannot be overstated, especially for those whose families may not be supportive and close-knit. I know I am incredibly privileged to have Sean, and to have parents, siblings, and friends who show up for me the way they do. In my work with people in recovery, I have seen firsthand how community connections can fill this role—the key, as always, is giving yourself permission to ask your community for what you need.

Beyond our relationships with others, anchors can appear in small and surprising ways on a daily basis—especially once you start to look for them. It could be a smile from a barista who always remembers your name, or the way your dad signs "Dad" at the end of every text message. It could be a novel that transports you to another realm, a new release from your favorite music artist, chuckling to your favorite meme account, a perfect sunset that bathes your living room in amber light, or a pot of soothing lavender tea. Anchors may vary in size and significance, but when it comes to finding glimmers of Hope in the dark, all are equal in power.

BECOME A BODY GRIEF ROLE MODEL

In addition to finding our anchors, looking to others for examples of perseverance can be a powerful tool for planting seeds of hope when we are feeling hopeless. We are biologically wired to be on the lookout for stories of people who are faced with seemingly insurmountable obstacles. In fact, many bestselling books and Oscar-winning movies are about humans embodying the dance of Hopelessness/ Hope, with the main protagonists acting as role models for our own moments of hopelessness and despair. Hearing these stories literally triggers a dopamine response that makes us pay attention; our body wants us to know how they overcome their challenges, as this will give us hope that we can do the same.

In our daily lives, we can find role models to look to as we navigate our own Hopelessness. One of my role models is the one and only Magic Marka, whom we met in chapter 6. I met Marka when I was in the process of applying for my mobility service dog. It was as if she came into my life at just the right time. For me, she is living proof that life keeps going, and that things are allowed to get better. I joke that she is like *Pocahontas*'s Mother Willow or a wise owl, because she is full of many lessons. To me, she embodies what it means to be with our Body Grief, no matter how much it hurts. Hearing her story has helped me to keep going. If she can do it, so can I.

A role model is someone you can confidently learn from and lean on symbolically and/or emotionally, as they have been where you are and truly "get it." They do not need to embody every bit of what you believe—that leads to putting people onto a pedestal and dehumanizing them, and we all make mistakes and have varying beliefs about the world. Sometimes, your role model has been there all along: it is the person you usually go to for advice.

Being a role model to others can also help us not only to find

Hope but purpose in our Hopelessness. Purpose can manifest in the grandiose, such as starting a nonprofit, as I did. It can be found in acts of service to others on this path. But it can equally be found in something as small as reminding yourself of your duty of care to your pets.

The concept of role models and purpose are a throughline in groups such as AA, where a person's sponsor becomes their personal role model—somebody who has been to rock bottom, has lived to tell the tale, and can offer tools and coping skills for the journey. Being a sponsor to others is an act of service that brings a sense of purpose after Hopelessness. Elsewhere, role models might be found in a friend group, in a professional setting, on social media, or in therapy/recovery groups.

BEWARE OF COMPARISON: YOUR STORY IS UNIQUE TO YOU

While inspiring role models help us focus on our strengths and remind us of what's possible, comparing ourselves to them can often compound our Hopelessness, leading to shame and deepening our Body Grief.

There is a fine line between inspiration and comparison. When we're inspired, we build self-compassion; our role model's stories help us see our strengths and reframe our perceived weaknesses. But when we're in comparison, we feel a growing sense of shame and find ourselves having thoughts such as *They may be suffering, but they can still do X, Y, and Z* and *I can't do that so I must be a failure.* You've likely heard the saying "Comparison is the thief of joy." But I would say that it can also poach our last bit of Hope if we don't stay aware.

Of course, comparison is not wrong in and of itself. It is an innate human tendency that helps us assess where we fit within a group. But in today's social media world, it's hard to know what's real and what's not, and all too easy to start comparing ourselves to others whose stories and images have been hyper-edited and filtered to attract the most follows and likes.

The most inspiring role models will be the ones who don't promise any miracles or pretend to have it all figured out, because they know this is how life is. They know that for every up, there will be more downs to come—and that this is okay. True inspiration simply offers the possibility that other storylines exist. Identifying with the way they have navigated life's inevitable challenges is what begins to kindle our Hope.

Exercise:

HOPEFUL ROLE MODEL INTERVIEW

To help you identify positive role models for going from hopeless to hopeful, I want you to identify a person in your life that you look up to and, if possible, ask for thirty minutes of their time. In my practice, I literally call this the "Interview Tool"—and it's one I've used to bring you all the stories I have included in this book! The purpose of this interview is to help you "live into" the experience of others whose story you identify with. Some questions to ask might include:

- What do you remind yourself when it feels like your body is betraying you?

- At what points in your journey have you felt hopeless?

- What do you do when you're feeling this way?

- What things bring you hope when it feels like all is lost?

- How has staying hopeful helped you push through in times of struggle?

If speaking to an actual person is not possible, then identify a public figure you look up to and try to identify what you see as their core values. Ask yourself, why is it that you look up to them? Do you think they ever feel hopeless? What have they shared about having faith in times of struggle? What parts of their story feel hopeful to you?

What Do You Need: A Fix or a Hug?

As we've seen, when we're deep in our Body Grief, it takes a lot of courage to ask for what we need, especially if we're no longer able to demonstrate what a good fighter we are. But when we are feeling hopeless, oftentimes the last thing we need is a solution, and what we really need is a hug. This can be hard enough to convey to ourselves, but it is usually even harder to convey to our loved ones who so desperately want to help.

For example, in my worst moments, Sean, a fixer at heart, wants nothing more than to see me free from pain. He will swoop in with offers of help and ideas for what to do next, but this has the opposite effect. Even after ten years together, it's hard for him to understand that often all I need from him is a hug, an embrace, a touch, a kiss, and the words "I'm so sorry this is happening, it is so unfair." With his fix-it approach, I am left feeling unsupported—and he is left feeling unhelpful. It's a lose-lose for the both of us.

This is not an uncommon phenomenon, especially when social gender norms are at play. Generally, men are socialized to push aside their feelings and focus on fixing things and moving on, whereas women are more likely to be socialized to feel comfortable experiencing the majority of our emotions (except anger, perhaps, as we saw in chapter 6) and to hold space for whatever is present (having the time for the latter, of course, being a function of privilege).

It was through therapy that Sean and I were finally able to understand the story behind our actions. I learned to see Sean's attempts to fix my Body Grief as his way of showing love, and Sean came to understand why his attempts to fix hurt me so much.

The truth is, I cannot be fixed. When he or anyone else tried to fix me, it felt to me like it was partly because they did not want to have to worry about my pain—that they did not care. Tied up in this, too, was the feeling that I had disappointed them by not being the Jayne they wanted me to be. What I wanted and needed, and still do, is unconditional support and a place to simply be seen and heard, without any pressure to "get better." What I needed, and still do, was compassion, a listening ear, a shoulder to cry on, laughter, food—and yes, the latest juicy gossip!

This is not to say that a desire to fix is inherently wrong. But the key is to express exactly what it is you need in the moment: a fix or a hug. A fix might look like advice, coming up with solutions, or focusing on potential positive outcomes. A hug could be, of course, an embrace or simply more direct eye contact, validation of what hurts, and the space to be heard. Given how solutions-oriented we are as a society in general, no wonder it can be harder to ask for the latter. Some helpful scripts in this scenario might be:

- "I know you're trying to be helpful, but I'd really love it if you could just listen to me vent right now."

- "I'm feeling sad right now and just want to watch a movie together. Can we do that?"

- "I already talked about this in therapy today. What I really need is to just take in the view and enjoy this meal with you."

Practice Self-Compassion

We can also ask ourselves whether we need a fix or a hug. Self-compassion is how we hug ourselves when we're feeling hopeless—a practice that is more complex than just repeating positive words in a mirror that you may or may not believe to be true (which only works if these words are filled with deep love for the hurting human being on the inside).

Self-compassion is an attempt to take care of that part of you that is feeling hopeless, the part of you that forgot how to be happy. This may look like cooking yourself your favorite meal, taking yourself out on a drive with the windows down and singing your heart out, journaling with your cat on your lap, or giving yourself a literal hug. And yes, it can also mean looking in the mirror and letting yourself know "Someday, I will feel Hope again." For this reason alone, self-compassion is a superpower for our Body Grief journey.

Practicing self-compassion isn't about toxic positivity or glossing over the reality of what is happening. It's about being kind to yourself, being soft, nurturing yourself, and aiming for each word and touch you give yourself to be filled with gratitude. Say you trip and sprain your ankle because you were looking down at your phone. Rather than blame yourself, having self-compassion would sound like "It's okay, I am allowed to be flawed and human, and I am grateful that I had the softness of my hips and thighs to catch my fall and protect me from further harm."

In fact, self-compassion and gratitude are close cousins. When I show myself compassion, I am simultaneously showing gratitude for my existence in this world—and so self-compassion becomes another powerful anchor. After all, we cannot hate ourselves or our body into becoming what we will be grateful for "someday." It may seem easier, but I promise you it won't work.

Play: A Reminder That Life Is for Living

In many ways, Hope is the truest form of self-preservation: it is what literally keeps us in this world when it feels like all is lost. One way that we can increase our capacity to stay in a hopeful state is to embrace *play* as a vital part of being with our Body Grief.

I know this may sound a little bit Pollyannaish; when we're feeling hopeless, play is often the last thing on our minds. But play helps us stay connected to the part of us that understands that life is for *living* and is therefore an essential part of any healing journey. No matter what we are experiencing in our body, we have a right to simply enjoy the experience of being here. Little kids know this, and one reason they naturally embrace play is that they haven't yet learned that they must "earn their keep" in this world. In a culture that rewards us for our productivity, activities that have no end result attached—like climbing trees, dressing up, and playing hide-and-seek—have no value and are therefore not encouraged.

For this reason, play is a concept that many of us find challenging to lean into as adults. The systems in which we live and work are not set up for us to find joy in doing something solely because it feels good. In fact, one reason so many of us use alcohol to relax is because we often need a drink to switch off the part of our brain that tells us we're not allowed to have fun. But I am here to tell you that this is not the case. Play in and of itself is calming our nervous system as it activates the frontal lobe, and therefore shuts off the fight, flight, freeze or fawn response (finally, the amygdala gets to rest!). It also nurtures your inner child and helps to heal the mind, body, and soul, making us happier and more content in the long run.

What do we even mean when we talk about play? At its core, play is anything that lights you up and helps you remember how good it feels to simply be alive. In practice, it can look like any activity that has no end result, like dancing, singing, coloring, drawing, or reading a novel. It might also literally mean playing a board game or creating your own game to play with friends or a pet. Play also is any activity, hobby, or creative pursuit where your mind can get lost. Recently, this has been in painting for me. Knitting colorful squares, just for the calming act of knitting itself, also became a go-to when I was feeling hopeless. Turns out my cat liked sitting on them, so I left them around the house for her like a crazy cat lady.

And speaking of animals, our furry friends can make the best playmates. Kate, whom we met at the beginning of this chapter, once told me that during a moment of deep Hopelessness her pup started rolling around in the snow, activating her inner child. She fell on the cold snowy ground next to him and started making snow angels for no reason other than because it just felt right—and as her arms waved up and down in the snow, Hope slowly seeped in.

"I am welcome here": Kendra's Story

I met Kendra through social media, after we were blessed by the "algorithm gods" and connected over our service dogs and chronic illnesses. When Kendra shared her story with me, I could feel the twin themes of Hopelessness and Hope interwoven in her words. To close this chapter, let's take a look at how she found the faith to keep going when it felt like all was lost; the anchors that helped her stay the course; and the roles that community, play, and role models have played in helping her find Hope.

The email read: "As far as your guest, I'm sorry to say we cannot accommodate her at this time." Since being diagnosed with celiac disease in 2017 while in her late forties, Kendra had become well-accustomed to this kind of message. "We also do not allow outside food, and suggest that your friend eat prior to arrival." Kendra felt her stomach drop. The email was from the winery she and her friends would be visiting to kick off their week-long girls' trip.

It was only a few hours later that she received another message, this time from the Airbnb they'd booked: they were unable to accommodate Kendra's gluten detection service dog, Suki—one of the anchors she relied on to help her live with her disease. And it was then that Kendra broke. She felt completely and utterly hopeless: these emails were just another reminder that her life and her choices would always be compromised by celiac.

The Americans with Disabilities Act (ADA) recognizes celiac disease as a disability, as it truly does disable those with the autoimmune disease. Kendra, who has dedicated much of the last seven years to healing her relationship with her Body Grief, explained why this is to me. Once a person with celiac ingests gluten, the immune system starts to attack what she describes as the "plush, shag carpet" of the villi of the small intestine.

As she puts it, "We need all that plush yarn to suck up the nutrients in our food. But for someone with celiac disease, it's like that plush shag carpet has become a smooth tile surface." This means you just don't get your nutrients, leading to malnourishment and disrupted gut function. But this is just one of the more than two hundred symptoms of celiac disease, including migraines, infertility, depression, anxiety, fatigue, joint pain, and even seizures.

Kendra called her friend and told her: "I think it may be best if I just stay home. I am only going to be a burden and weigh everyone else down." Here, we see Hopelessness quickly morph into Apology. Sometimes taking up space just felt like too much effort, despite everything she advocated for online. Just going out to eat had become an ordeal that colored every single aspect of her life. Living with celiac was exhausting.

Once, she had unknowingly taken two antibiotic pills with a touch of gluten in them and had been sick with sores and blisters in her mouth and throat, swollen joints, brain fog, gastrointestinal upsets, headaches, and full body chills for two whole weeks. Other times, she felt deeply ashamed of having to explain her digestive issues and bathroom habits to strangers who wanted to know why she couldn't eat or drink certain things. It all felt so unfair. This trip was just another reminder of how draining it was, and how Hopeless she felt, living with this disease.

But on the other end of the line, Kendra's friend refused her request to bow out of the girls' trip. "Do not talk to my friend that way!" she chimed in. Kendra smirked; her friend's joke was the glimmer of Hope that would pull her out of this despair. "We will make this work," the friend went on.

That friend called ahead to every restaurant and outing, responded to every email, and sourced alternative options. Watching her, Kendra was able to have faith that her needs would be met, no matter how "inconvenient" this felt. She began to feel as welcome as everybody else. Her friend also became a powerful role model for Kendra: by taking it upon herself to ensure that Kendra's needs were always taken care of, she was modeling that it was okay for Kendra to do the same for herself. Kendra began to feel hope.

That one trip inspired Kendra to start traveling more, and to see the importance of educating restaurants on how to accommodate people with celiac disease. She also started sharing her discoveries of places that are celiac-friendly online, which helped her start to build community with others living with the disease. In this, Kendra has become a role model to others for how to live with celiac shame-free.

The limitations of the disease have also helped her discover a passion for cooking, as she has challenged herself to discover just how good gluten-free food can be. Rather than feel Hopeless about not having her needs met, or the fact she will never "get back" the options that were open to her before she got sick, playing with ingredients in the kitchen has helped her discover delicious, gluten-free options that everybody wants to eat.

She even gained the courage to bring gluten-free creations to dinner parties where she no longer feels the need to disclose her illness. That freedom alone brings hope with her Body Grief journey, along with finding community through "Yappy Hour" at her local dog park, gatherings which have become another anchor for her. Bringing gluten-free food to parties and attending these meetups with her service dog are ways for Kendra to integrate with her local community versus hiding away and feeling like she will never fully be able to join in. These days, Kendra has taken her illness and her Body Grief by the reins and looks for pockets of joy wherever she can find them—like watching Suki rough and tumble with her best dog friend, Navi.

⟜

If you have taken anything from this chapter, I hope it's that staying with your Body Grief, even in the depths of Hopelessness, is the way you move forward in your journey. I *know* how hard it is to hold blind faith that things will get better when it feels like all is lost—but as you have seen, glimmers of Hope can show up even when we are experiencing the lowest of lows. After all, there is no light without the dark, and no dark without the light. Trusting this means having the courage to keep moving toward healing, one step at a time. Finding your anchors, building and nurturing a community, losing yourself and finding moments of joy in play, and looking to your Body Grief role model are all vital supports for this part of the journey. And perhaps most important of all, using these tools to help you keep the faith will also keep returning you into the loving arms of Body Trust.

AFFIRMATIONS

"I am brave."

"I am strong and soft."

"I am human and flawed."

"I will survive this."

"I am proud of my body and my mind."

"I am worthy of connection and happiness."

JOURNAL PROMPT

What are your anchors? List all your reasons to be here, from your biggest hopes and dreams for yourself and your loved ones to your daily cup of coffee. As time goes on, keep adding to the list. Read it every time you are feeling hopeless.

NINE

Body Trust:
I Believe in Me

The fluorescent lights of the gastrointestinal doctor's office flickered, and Indie Lee took a deep breath to ground herself. This was certainly not her first rodeo when it came to invasive medical procedures. Over the past eighteen years, she had faced a series of life-threatening diagnoses, including pancreatitis, brain tumors that cannot be explained, and severe rheumatoid arthritis. Now it had been Indie herself who had advocated for this colonoscopy. She has a family history of liver and bile duct cancer, and she wasn't taking any chances. Her RA medication also hadn't been working, and she'd been experiencing lots of inflammation, pain in her abdomen, and a loss of appetite, leading her to worry that something wasn't right with her digestive system.

Years back, Indie had started a skin care company to highlight how the things we put on our skin affect our entire body, and after all she'd been through with her health, she was very connected to her bodily cues. She knew now her body was trying to tell her something.

The doctor knocked on the door and came in.

"Everything looks good, Mrs. Lee, but when were you going to tell me you have Crohn's disease?"

Indie chuckled, but her eyes were not laughing. "I'm sorry, I don't know what you mean," she said. "I don't have Crohn's."

The doctor replied, "I beg to differ. I was just all up in your business and I can confirm that you certainly do."

A large exhale escaped from Indie's lungs as if she was being deflated. *Here we go again*, she thought. By this point, she had cycled through Dismissal, Shock, Apology, Fault, Fight, and Hopelessness countless times, and she found herself bracing for yet another encounter with Body Grief, another cycle of heartbreak. Yet, at that moment, she also felt the steady presence of Body Trust. As her past experiences flashed in front of her eyes, she realized that it was precisely *because* she had been here so many times that she was able to trust that whatever this new diagnosis held, she would be able to get through it in a safe, healthy way. After all, her body had shown her yet again that it was always on her side—it was listening to her body's small whispers that had pushed her to advocate for a colonoscopy.

Now that Indie had been diagnosed with Crohn's, she and her medical team could come up with a treatment plan, preventing further damage from being done. She also had clear evidence as to why her rheumatoid arthritis flares weren't calming down with her current medication: she wasn't treating the other underlying autoimmune disease that was at play, Crohn's. Trusting in her body had saved her—just as it had saved her many times before.

At that moment, Indie felt so grateful for her Body Grief. She had lived in this body for over half a century, and for the past eighteen years it had felt like it was under attack from itself. The Perceived Body Betrayal had been intense. But she was done blaming her body, and she was done feeling crazy for listening to it and advocating for what she needed. Experience had shown her, time and again, that she could trust her body and her intuition. Rather than a sign of defeat, Indie's exhale was her acceptance that although the process was starting all over again, she could depend on her hard-won Body Trust to guide her through it.

This Is Body Trust

So here we are at Body Trust. We feel attuned and at one with our body. We are able to listen to our body and give it what it needs, safe in the knowledge that our body is on our side. We hold space for healing, ease, and attunement with our body and its needs, lifting the fog and helping us keep the faith.

Body Trust comes knocking when we have burned out on the phases of the Body Grief that do not serve us and are maladaptive to our healing. In these moments—moments that often arrive on the heels of Hope—we are reminded that our mind, body, soul, and spirit are stronger when they are working together. Hope provides a glimpse into the future, reminding us that there is always more to live for. This in turn opens the door to Body Trust, which asks us to have faith in our body in the present moment.

Let's take a deeper look at the characteristics of this phase, the better to recognize and appreciate when we are in it.

BODY TRUST IS INNATE

As infants, before we have language, we have no option but to trust in the nonverbal cues our body sends us. Our body lets us know when to eat, when to sleep, when to poop, and when we need a hug—and at that age, that's pretty much all we need to know! But as we mature and language takes over, we discover all sorts of ways to override our innate bodily needs. Rather than taking a nap when we're tired, we caffeinate. Our stomach growls at us, and instead of taking time to sit down and eat a proper lunch, we have another coffee or grab a protein bar on the go. We feel uncomfortable in a social situation, so we chug another glass of wine.

We disrupt our Body Trust on the daily, but our body never stops communicating with us. Speaking in both physical sensations and emotions, it signals to us when something needs our attention—be this a physical need or ailment that needs tending to, or when something it wants and needs is being presented to us and it wants us to say yes to it. Body Trust arises when we respond to the subtle and not so subtle cues our body sends us. In this mind-body-spirit conversation with our body, we are able to relax into whatever we are experiencing in the moment.

BODY TRUST IS INTUITIVE

Because our body is always speaking to us, we come back to Body Trust anytime we are able to lean into our intuition. In the grips of Body Grief, this often means overriding social and cultural conditioning telling us our body is "defective" or that it has "failed us," fueling Perceived Body Betrayal. But being *with* each phase of our Body Grief process helps rebuild trust in our body, expanding our overall capacity for Body Trust so that we can start living from this place again.

BODY TRUST MEANS BEING OKAY WITH NOT BEING OKAY

For Indie, Body Trust meant knowing she could be okay with not being okay—something that we both agree needs to be normalized. Living in a body is *hard*, especially when that body has experienced multiple ailments and other losses. In fact, it is much more normal *not* to be okay than it is for everything to be working perfectly all the time. Pretending everything is fine brings us right back to Dismissal, the phase that often signals the beginning of the Body Grief process. When your reality is that you are *not* okay, one way to build Body Trust is to learn to be at peace with this.

BODY TRUST IS A TWO-WAY STREET

In order for you to be able to trust your body, your body needs to be able to trust you. This means facing your Body Grief head-on, feeling whatever feelings come with this, and continuously advocating for whatever it is you need. In practice, this could look like taking time off work to rest when you're sick, instead of pushing through. It may mean acknowledging that your body has been experiencing a particular symptom and making a doctor's appointment to get checked out. Or it could be as simple as making time to eat breakfast in the morning and making sure you pack lunch for work, to prevent your blood sugar from crashing in the afternoon. In all of this, you show your body that you are on its side, building Body Trust.

Signs You Are in Body Trust

You are listening to and honoring your bodily cues.

You are setting boundaries with yourself.

You are feeling your feelings.

You are practicing self-care.

You feel confident in your ability to heal, no matter how messy it is.

BODY TRUST IS A MINDSET, NOT A DESTINATION

It's important to remember that Body Trust is not the end goal of the Body Grief process. Instead, it is a skill we can develop as we engage more deeply with our Body Grief, and one that can become an ally as we cycle through all the other phases. Body Trust feels like an unclenching of the jaw and fists as the tension is slowly released from the body. When we are in Body Trust, the mind, body, and spirit are finally on the same page, and we know that we have the inner and outer resources to endure what is to come.

BODY TRUST HELPS US MOVE THROUGH EACH PHASE OF BODY GRIEF

But Body Trust also makes us feel vulnerable. Body Trust must be earned, but it can be lost again in an instant with each new diagnosis, accident, breakdown of bodily functions, or flare-up. This is what makes experience and hindsight so valuable. As we saw in Indie's story, it was her ability to reflect on her previous experiences within each phase of Body Grief that helped her lean into Body Trust when she received her new diagnosis. This process is exactly what you have learned to do throughout this book, as I have helped you fully be with each part of your Body Grief and to allow the process to flow.

Building Body Trust is not about perfection, speed, or form; it is about consistently showing up and proving to yourself that you can and will survive as you continue to learn new coping tools along the way. With each step you take into the Ocean of Body Awareness, you are immersing yourself in Body Trust, and hopefully finding a little bit of peace to carry with you. When we are in Body Trust, the judgment and mean-spirited inner thoughts fade away. There is no name-calling or inner bullying; instead, we discover that so much of Body Trust is about forgiveness. Forgiveness for the blame and shame our body has been subjected to. For the constant tug-of-war between pushing our body to the limit and it never being strong enough. Forgiveness for berating our body for not being perfect, and for the lack of kindness we have shown it. Forgiveness for not expressing our gratitude to our body for all the ways it has been trying to keep us afloat.

In this way, Body Trust is both a phase of Body Grief *and* an ally throughout the entire process.

When we are in Dismissal, Body Trust fosters self-advocacy.

When we are in Shock, Body Trust fosters self-regulation.

When we are in Apology, Body Trust fosters self-esteem.

When we are in Fault, Body Trust fosters self-forgiveness.

When we are in Fight, Body Trust fosters self-acceptance.

When we are Hopeless, Body Trust helps us keep the faith.

Reflection

Take a moment here to close your eyes and breathe, inhaling through your nose and exhaling through your mouth. Notice yourself constantly recycling that breath, in the same way that your Body Grief moves through its own cycles to find its way back to Body Trust. As you wiggle your toes and guide yourself into the Ocean of Body Awareness, notice how it feels to be in a body that you not only trust, but that trusts you back.

How does it feel to know that you are always supported, even when you aren't "whole"? What emotion arises when you realize that your body has shown up for you in the darkest of times, and in the best of times? What specific sensations do you feel in your body right now as you embody trust? As you acknowledge the sensation of Body Trust, remind yourself that this is not a destination. This is a port, a safe harbor that you will visit time and again on your Body Grief journey.

What Disrupts Our Capacity for Body Trust

Earlier, we learned that Body Trust is innate, an instinct we are born with. Yet over time we unlearn this trust, as the natural mind-body connection is eroded by what I call Body Trust Disruptors.

Body Trust Disruptors are anything that makes us question our intuition or impedes us from hearing our innate bodily cues, and they come at us thick and fast from the moment we are born. As we have learned, as infants, we have no option but to trust what our body is communicating to us, and to put this trust in the hands of our primary caregivers. In an ideal world, these caregivers are attuned to us and help us respond to our bodily cues as they arise. But parents and/or guardians don't always give their children everything they need. Sometimes it's because they lack access to resources, often due to systems of oppression. In other situations, this can be due to mental health struggles, such as postpartum depression, financial burdens, or physical disabilities. Or perhaps our parents were not properly parented themselves, and so they never learned how. No matter the reason, our innate Body Trust is often disrupted early on.

As soon as we venture outside of the home, we come face-to-face with social and cultural attitudes that further disrupt our sense of trust in our body, from racism and sexism to ableism. Being judged as less-than or even being abused because of the body we are in can ignite a trauma response, creating the opposite of Body Trust. Now, instead of feeling at one with our body, we turn against it as we try to make our body fit the mold of what is deemed "acceptable" or "safe," according to body size or shape, race, ability, age, sex, or gender. The more society tells us that we don't fit, the less we are able to trust in our body.

We may also encounter Body Trust Disruptors when we experience events that cause unexpected harm to our bodies and well-being, often in a way that's outside of our control. These can include an unexcepted sickness, mental illness, assault, a car accident, or medical malpractice. In some instances, these disruptors may have their roots in classism and economic inequality—as illustrated in many of the stories in this book.

But sometimes, Body Trust Disruptors turn out to be necessary for our survival—and this is where Body Trust gets even more essential.

For instance, medication can disrupt our natural bodily cues, appetite, sleep, and digestion being three important areas that are often impacted. Once these cues are disrupted, it can be hard to feel at peace in our body and trust what it is telling us, even when we know the medicine is working for us. But this doesn't mean we can't give our body what it needs. It just becomes more complex.

I know from personal experience that leaning into Body Trust when starting a new medication or treatment plan can be both daunting and exhausting. Some meds work, some do not, but almost all of them have adverse side effects. Body Trust comes into play when balancing these side effects with the benefits of the medication. For instance, when I was put on immunosuppressants after my immune system began rejecting the hardware that had been placed in my body, it was quite literally a hard pill to swallow, as my appetite disappeared and I was constantly nauseous or vomiting. My risk of lymphoma also increased significantly. And yet I was grateful for it all, because without this medication I would be in the hospital nonstop due to inflammation and other allergic reactions.

This is one small example of how confusing it can be when a drug that is quite literally keeping us alive simultaneously feels like it is slowly killing us. Talk about a leap of faith! In this scenario, Body Trust is knowing that no matter how I feel, I must eat *and* I must take my medicine twice a day. With this compromise, I am helping my body to trust that I will do anything to keep it alive, while acknowledging that any adverse side effects are my body doing the same for me.

In the same way, we know that our body needs food to survive, and so we learn to nourish ourselves even if we don't have an appetite. We know that our body needs sleep, and so if our normal sleep pattern is disrupted, we may need to work on creating a supportive bedtime routine and learn to rest as and when we can.

STANCE'S STORY: DISRUPTING THE
BODY TRUST DISRUPTORS

Learning to give our body what it needs—even when grappling with Body Trust Disruptors—is a profound example of Body Trust in action, and an increased ability to attune to our body in this way is "proof" that we are working with our Body Grief. This is something Stance had to learn the hard way after she agreed to weight-loss surgery as part of her eating disorder story, a story that began for her in fifth grade.

"I can't remember a time when my body was not a problem," she remembers. "Because I was in a bigger body, changing my body was the focal point of my childhood, and it became the focus of my life."

Stance entered treatment for her eating disorder after a traumatic sexual assault in her freshman year of college caused her binge eating disorder to ramp up. Unfortunately, she only encountered more of the same fatphobia in the treatment center, something that is sadly not uncommon. All of a sudden, she found herself in a room with a bunch of women in smaller bodies who had been diagnosed with anorexia and bulimia, eating disorders that were more commonly understood at the time. These women were praised and celebrated when they gained weight.

But being in a larger body, Stance discovered that she was not allowed to talk about her desire to be smaller. Her now-recovered self understands that the attitudes she encountered there could be considered malpractice, since individuals with eating disorders exist in all shapes and sizes. But at the time, it felt like the very system she had turned to for help had silenced her. As a result, she left treatment feeling even more distrustful of her body and carrying even heavier Body Grief. Stance was never given the proper space to process her Body Grief, her internalized fatphobia, or her lack of Body Trust.

This led to Stance seeking a referral to a weight-loss surgeon once she was discharged from the treatment center. Even she was shocked when she passed the psychiatric assessment and was given the go-ahead to undergo permanent gastric sleeve surgery. She knew she was still sick, and she was about to embark on a procedure where 70 percent of your stomach is removed, severely limiting the amount of food you are physically able to consume. Talk about a Body Trust Disruptor. The surgery was essentially a medical intervention she was advised to turn to because she could not be trusted to listen to her own hunger cues.

For the first six weeks following the surgery, Stance was put on a liquid diet, which she describes as jump-starting the process of her binge eating disorder shifting into anorexia. To her delight, she discovered that she no longer had hunger cues. Soon, she was exercising on a daily basis while eating less than a toddler. She also had very little medical supervision. "I felt like I was getting away with murder, and yet it was allowed," she later told me.

Now Stance was losing weight rapidly, but rather than being healed, she was thinking even more obsessively about her body. This was reinforced by the praise she began to receive about her shape. Finally, her body fit the mold of what was sexy and powerful. Finally, she felt worthy. She was doing everything the doctors told her to and doing it well. And because she "looked good," nobody was worried—even when her hair began to fall out and her labs started showing that she was badly malnourished and needed injections of vitamins.

Stance had put her trust in the system that was meant to help her heal her eating disorder. But the treatment she received was all delivered through a fatphobic, healthist, and ableist lens, which only served to further erode the innate Body Trust that had already been disrupted by her eating disorder and assault.

It wasn't until she experienced a breakup that Stance realized her body and her size had never been the issue; it was the impact of all these isms that had made her sick. Her partner had previously aspired to be a weight-loss surgeon and had constantly praised her for her weight loss post-surgery while also repeatedly mentioning how she was the curviest woman he had ever been with. By the time he broke up with her, Stance was withering away to almost nothing, and still she wasn't good enough for him.

It was like a switch flipped in her brain, and she decided it was finally time to trust in her body again. In fact, it had never been about her body. Her body was not an object, but it had been treated that way by her therapists, her doctors, and her ex. In some ways it was the Shock of the breakup that opened her eyes to the way forward: only through rebuilding Body Trust would she find happiness and healing.

The diet culture that Stance had been indoctrinated into at such a young age, the sexual assault, the attitudes she encountered at the treatment center, and the gastric sleeve itself had all been Body Trust Disruptors, and Stance experienced yet more Body Grief as she slowly came to terms with this. For example, living with the gastric sleeve is not easy. Stance will never be able to stomach normal-size meals without getting sick, and she can't eat and drink at the same time. This means she has to stay incredibly diligent with her nutrition and have small meals and snacks throughout the day or she will fall short on nourishment. But this has in fact helped her build Body Trust, as it has meant learning to really listen to her body again. Having flexibility, compassion, and patience for and with her body have been key to her recovery.

For Stance, this has meant learning to live with the Body Trust Disruptor that has literally been placed in her body. It has meant learning how to manage her pain while simultaneously nourishing her body and living her life to the fullest. Today, Stance exists with her body and her Body Grief every day, and she is coping and healing and living and fostering Body Trust every step of the way.

Exercise:

NOTICE YOUR ENERGY

So much of Body Trust is about truly getting to know your body so that you can become better attuned to the nonverbal cues it uses to communicate with you. One way to practice this is to pay attention to how you feel in varying spaces and situations and during certain experiences. Energy cannot be denied. We transfer energy to one another with every word and every touch, and understanding how our bodies react and how the energy shifts in our bodies as we engage with the world is incredibly helpful for developing Body Trust.

To practice this right now, imagine being at a football game or a concert at a moment when the crowd goes wild with joy. Feel the energy in your body shift as you visualize this; most likely your heart will start beating faster, you may get goose bumps or feel a fluttering in your stomach. Now imagine sitting down to take an exam. What sensations are present as the energy in your body shifts? That right there, that shift, is what I want you to focus on. It is learning to pay attention to the fluctuations of energy in your body, without labeling anything "right" or "wrong," that will help you start to speak its language more fluently.

When practicing this out in the world, simply stay curious, taking inventory of what your body wants you to know. When you can start to act on this knowing is how you start flexing the Body Trust muscle.

The Never-Ending Work of Building Body Trust

At the end of the day, Body Trust is a practice, one that we expand our capacity for by being present in each phase of the Body Grief process. But there are specific tools you can use to build Body Trust. As always, these tools are meant to be adapted to your specific circumstances and will be applicable at various stages of your Body Grief journey.

PRACTICE TRUE SELF-CARE

One way to build Body Trust is through self-care. We often hear self-care being discussed as an indulgence or an escape, something that is used to numb out and avoid facing reality rather than an empowering practice. If this is how you have come to view self-care, I highly encourage you to rewire your thinking. Yes, as with so many things in life, self-care has been co-opted by capitalist interests that want to sell us ways to "feel good." But prioritizing care for yourself is foundational to strengthening the mind-body connection that is at the heart of Body Trust.

True self-care is laying down a cushion on the good days so that on the not-so-good days you have something to fall back on. Creating this padding through our self-care practices is much simpler than you may have been led to think. There are layers and levels to self-care, beginning with simply allowing ourselves to honor our bodily cues: eating when we are hungry, crying when we are sad, sleeping when we are tired, laughing when we are elated. This is self-care in its most basic form.

The next level up is hygiene: taking a shower, brushing your teeth, and perhaps putting on some lipstick or aftershave to add a little sparkle to your day. Now you are ready to layer on some walks in the sun, an extra five minutes in the car with your coffee before going into work, taking an extra lap in the pool, or adding an extra dollop of whipped cream to your ice cream sundae. Other examples of self-care at this layer might include:

- Regular calls with a trusted friend.

- Not pushing yourself on days when you are exhausted, even if this means letting others down.

- Deepening your spiritual studies and/or practices.

- Cleaning up your social media and unfollowing accounts that promote envy, comparison, or toxic positivity.

- Trying out new recipes.

- Taking a nap with your pet.

- Learning a new skill, such as knitting, twerking, getting into vinyl, origami, or even a new language.

- If you're feeling really inspired, you might try a self-care game I sometimes play with my loved ones: name an emotion, and then play a song that reminds you of that emotion. It could be a throwback or a song you've never even heard before.

Regularly giving our body what it needs—whether that's our favorite food, a hot bath, or a few hours reading a racy romance novel—lets our body know that we are on its side. As we have seen, Body Trust is a two-way street, and with our self-care practices, we are communicating to our body, "I see you, I got you, I love you."

REGULATE YOUR NERVOUS SYSTEM

As we are pulled in unanticipated directions by what our body is experiencing, each phase of Body Grief can disrupt our central nervous system. Specific tools of nervous system regulation include grounding, deep breathing, meditation, and self-soothing actions, such as rolling your shoulders back and away from your ears, rubbing your feet together (called "cricketing," how cute!), aromatherapy, listening to soothing music, self-massage, and stretching. These tools help bring the frontal lobe back online, welcoming our rational thoughts back into the conversation and reestablishing a two-way conversation with our body.

Once we regulate the nervous system, we are able to assess whatever our situation is with a full understanding of our history and what our body has been through. We are able to see through the fog of anxiety to advocate for what will actually be supportive to our healing. We are also primed to listen to the more subtle, and often more supportive, whispers from within. In cases like these, intuition *plus* intellect is the magic formula for building Body Trust.

TRUST OTHERS: HEALTHY CODEPENDENCY

Throughout our Body Grief journey, there will be times when we have no choice but to put our trust in others. This dynamic is there in all caregiver relationships, from medical professionals and partners to service animals and family members. We know how hard it can be to trust others, especially when we have been ignored, dismissed, let down, or even harmed in our Body Grief. The good news is that developing Body Trust in and with ourselves can also help us develop trust in these relationships.

The reality is, we need others. Yet codependence is another C-word that has gotten a bad rep—partly because we are so deeply conditioned not to need others. It is seen as dangerous and weak to rely too heavily on any one person, group, or organization. Yes, this dynamic *can* become toxic when an unequal power dynamic between the individuals involved paves the way for abuses of power, like when a partner controls the household finances as a way to control their spouse (also known as financial abuse). And on a societal level, access to healthcare being tied to a person's employment status can be a way for companies to control their workers.

But the answer is not to never need anybody for anything. Healthy codependence goes hand in hand with Body Trust, because putting our trust in others lets our body know that we are not alone in our Body Grief, which helps us stay out of Apology and be okay with asking others to accommodate us and our needs. Our body will not always be able to let us know when a person is trustworthy or not. It may give us cues to a new person that contain the echo of unresolved grievances from our past, and it is important to proceed with caution when creating new connections as we feel slowly into the difference between our intuition and the chemical reaction of fight, flight, freeze, or fawn. But this, again, is a practice.

As we've learned, trust must always be earned and can only ever be built over time. Healthy codependency looks like having high levels of empathy and compassion for another person and acknowledging that they are only human while also leaning into their support in times of need. It may look like a disabled person and their mobility aids, two friends who share a deep connection, a mother and newborn, a person who identifies as neurodivergent and a fidget toy while they "stim," an in-home caretaker, or medication.

Building healthy codependency takes patience and time, two qualities that help build Body Trust in and of themselves. Being patient and taking our time to get to know a person or practice that we are being asked to trust allows space for us to ease into vulnerability. This is especially important if our trust has been broken in the past, as it lets our body know that we are exercising caution when it comes to who and what we entrust with our care.

To the contrary, toxic codependency is usually accompanied by feelings of emptiness, feelings of being unwanted, feelings of abandonment, and not knowing or understanding the limits and boundaries of a person's love. Understanding and learning how to differentiate between healthy versus toxic codependency is key to building trust with others as well as within yourself.

SURRENDER: LETTING GO OF YOUR NEED FOR CONTROL

So much of the Body Grief journey is about accepting what is happening in our body, accepting that we are not in control, and perhaps, above all, accepting that life is not fair. This truly sucks—but it is the Truth (yes, with a capital *T*!). The more we can surrender to this reality and simply show up for our body and our life, the more we start to trust that while we might not always get what we want, we will always have everything we need.

If this thought freaks you out, I get it. Surrender is scary as hell, and I am not going to pretend otherwise. Surrender can be dismissed as "giving up" or "giving in," and as we know, everybody loves a fighter. But it is only through surrender that we get to experience truly living in the moment, trusting in the mind-body-spirit connection that we were born with. Surrender is terrifying and elating all at the same time because it allows us to accept our body and our life exactly as it is.

However, it isn't safe to surrender before we are ready. The same way a trust fall exercise only works when we know there is a group of friendly humans waiting to catch us, it is on us to do the work of creating an external and internal safety net so that we are able to *let go* and *go with* the waves of our Body Grief. Throughout this book, I have spoken many times about the need to accept where our body is at, and to learn to be with what is. But in truth, we often only reach this place when we have cycled through each phase of the Body Grief process. Accepting our body, wherever it is at, is what helps us believe in our body and its innate capacity to keep showing up. This is what helps us gather the external and internal resources we need for the ride.

For me, my safety net includes my comprehensive medical team, my service dog, medication, a regular self-care practice, and my Body Grief community. I also find safety in being willing to learn from my experiences and to always trust my intuition and advocate for what I need. For you, it might look like your yoga group, a book club, a therapist, or the ones you call your chosen family.

When we've cycled through each phase of the Body Grief process and have arrived at Body Trust, surrender becomes the most freeing feeling in the world. In many ways, Body Trust is a form of surrender in and of itself. It shows that we are ready to have faith and trust completely in whatever process is unfolding. Can you already feel how empowering this is? Surrender doesn't mean game over. It proves how resilient we have become in our Body Grief.

Honestly, I never thought I would feel safe enough to surrender. It pains me to think about the days I spent scrambling for answers on the internet while rejecting my body's cues to rest, heal, and resign from Fight or Fault. In those moments, I was fighting my body's natural healing process, taking emails while healing from a lumbar puncture and spinal leak, and planning my pain meds around my client calls. But I also have compassion for that Jayne. She was scared, and she didn't know any better. It is because of the lessons learned in those experiences that I find myself where I am today.

Being at Peace with What Is

It dawned on me recently that I have never cried or shed a tear because of the physical pain I have experienced in my Body Grief. Instead, my tears have all sprung from Hopelessness and my fear that it will be this way forever. For me, leaning into Body Trust has meant surrendering to the fact that I can trust my body, I can trust my team, I can trust my tools, and I can surrender to this process, a process that I accept will include tears, pain, breakdowns and breakthroughs, and many glimmers of hope, because this is being in a body, and it is never-ending.

As humans, we are constantly fighting the aging process, but for what? For fear of death, or for fear that we will miss out on living? Perhaps we wouldn't be so fearful of our bodies aging and changing if we could learn to trust, if we could surrender to the Body Grief process and enjoy the life we are living *right now*, rather than waste our precious life-force energy fearing what is to come.

As I reflect on my own journey today, I know I would be stuck in the grips of my eating disorder had I not learned how to process my Body Grief. In fact, I might not be alive to tell this tale. What I learned in my eating disorder recovery is what gave me the resilience to safely move through the grief of the past five years. The seven phases of Body Grief are the sails that set us off on the Ocean of Body Awareness so we can safely tread these waters while slowly letting go of our need to be in control.

At age thirty-two, I feel like I am part Barbie, part Mrs. Potato

Head. Falling apart, limb by limb, all I can do is surrender to my Body Grief as the world moves on and I try to find where I fit in along the way. The other day, as I was delicately rinsing the suds from the scars that crisscross my soft lower belly, I realized it had been almost a year since my womb was removed. I sat in my shower chair embracing my rolls, my stretch marks, taking in every nook and cranny as if it were all a map of my Body Grief. At that moment, I thanked my body for being the keeper of my pain, the keeper of my grief, and the keeper of my healing. And as I lifted my arms to rinse the conditioner from my hair, my arms went numb, my spine tingling as my head went hazy.

I knew this meant I was about to faint; my body had sent me these signals before, I could trust them. And so, I put my head between my knees and called for Wheatie, who came immediately. I asked him to "brace," and he was able to help me safely out of the shower. Then I asked him for "help," and he immediately went to alert Sean. Sean came into the bedroom to check on me. I lay down and gave him the thumbs-up, signaling I was all good. Then he kissed me on the forehead and left me and Wheatie to just be.

Earlier that week, my immunologist refilled my immunosuppressants and immunoglobulin infusions to counteract my immune system response to the hardware that still lives in my body. We discussed the risk of further surgeries to remove the metal that my body continues to reject. I also had an MRI scheduled for my dislocated shoulder, and weekly visits from my physical therapist filled my calendar; I was coming to a more comprehensive understanding of the prognosis of my degenerative disease. This was my reality—and at that moment I was able to lean into Body Trust, to surrender, knowing I had all my tools in place to support myself within each phase of my Body Grief. At that moment, I was okay with not being okay.

Wheatie jumped up on the bed with my medication in his mouth.

I took a deep breath. I hadn't taken anything to manage my pain today, and he could tell by the way I was breathing that I was hurting. Because Body Trust doesn't take away our pain—but it does help us to handle it.

Lying there, that same paraphrased Taylor Swift lyric kept playing in my head: "I wasn't be sure this pain would be forevermore." Feeling connected to the emotions captured in the song sparked a glimmer of Hope that again brought me back to Body Trust.

If I want to leave you with anything here, it's this: we do not come out of the Body Grief process "fixed." Being human and living in a body means there will always be one more *thing*. One more change in how we experience our body, one more loss. But with the inner and outer resources, with hindsight, with adaptive coping tools, with compassion, and above all with Body Trust, we have everything we need to keep going, to keep living.

I thanked Wheatie and took my medication as I breathed deeply and grounded my body on the bed. After a while, I got in my wheelchair and put on some vinyl. With Sean's NFL game playing in the background, it was the start of another sweet evening with my little family. Feeling the music wash over me, I closed my eyes, took a deep breath, and told my body, "Thank you." Because even with all this Body Grief, I know that I can trust her.

AFFIRMATIONS

"This is Body Grief."

"It is okay for me to be in pain."

"I am willing to listen to my body."

"I am exactly where I need to be right now."

"I got you, body."

JOURNAL PROMPT

Free-write two to three pages using the following starting point: "Today, my body is telling me . . ."

Conclusion

Dear Reader,

People often ask me, "How do you do this? How do you keep such a positive attitude with all of your Body Grief?" Hopefully, now having read the book, you will know this is not easy for me. But with these last words, I want to offer a few hopeful reminders as you continue on your Body Grief journey.

If your body speaks to you, listen. That pain in your back that "just doesn't feel right"? Do yourself a favor and mention it to your doctor. Those ruminating thoughts about not being worthy? Share them with a friend. You are not alone, and your body is giving you these whispers because it needs a little help.

Lean into your community. Body Grief isolates us, and community is the antidote, as well as being a beautiful rebellion against the isms of the world—which seek to keep us separated from ourselves and from each other.

Use your privilege. Everybody reading this book holds some level of privilege, and the more privilege we have, the more we need to use it for good. The more we recognize our internalized isms, the more we heal ourselves, and therefore others.

Feelings are for *FEEL*ing, so fucking feel them, baby! And I mean ALL of them! I have filled this book with ways to securely feel your emotions, but this takes time and practice, so be gentle, patient, and compassionate with yourself. If you feel like you need it, don't hesitate to ask for help or reach out to a professional.

Romanticize your life. That sun shining through the window as you sip your morning coffee? Allow the universe to caress your soul and warm your heart while you take a deep inhale, savoring the notes of your French roast before you embark on another Monday morning adventure.

Allow yourself to find these pockets of joy in the most minuscule of ways. The flirty look your significant other shoots you when you pass by, the smell and feeling of a new book in your hands, waiting to be read. These are the moments that will help you find hope in the midst of your Body Grief.

Grief must exist alongside gratitude, or you will end up in a dark place. Sometimes this might sound as simple as "I am grateful for waking up." Other times, it might sound like "I am grateful for everything my body has gone through to get me here." Or it might be "I am grateful for this joint, for the adorable family of raccoons that moved into the tree in my backyard, and for the fresh canvas I am emoting my raw feelings onto through vibrant paints and theatrical brushstrokes, while blasting Celine Dion's greatest hits (maybe that last one's just me).

Above all, remember that life is fragile, and so it is precious. So take it slow, and remind yourself that you are doing the work simply by leaning into the compassionate healing process that is moving through Body Grief and into Body Trust.

I am so fucking proud of you. This is an imperfect journey, and you are doing it. Look at you! Look at us!

With gratitude,
Jayne

Acknowledgments

As you very well know by now, I am honest to a fault, and I must say I am still pinching myself.

This still doesn't feel real, that I, Jayne, who struggled to read until I was in the third grade, am now a published author. That I, Jayne, who was dismissed for years, not only by herself, but by therapists and doctors, am now helping others find ways to heal their own Body Grief. I can't help but find myself reflecting on the journey that made it all possible. One deeply enriched by the contributions and courage of so many individuals throughout this entire journey. This work is a tapestry woven from the threads of countless stories of Grief, trauma, and life experiences, and I am so thankful to each and every storyteller and contributor in this beautiful creation. That little girl who struggled with reading and who was gaslit countless times is now here to help amplify other's voices, and other's stories, because we all deserve to heal.

Truly none of this would have been possible without my amazing book doula, Ruby Warrington, author of *Sober Curious* and *Women Without Kids*. I like to call her my Magical Unicorn. We met in the most serendipitous of ways, and I could not be more grateful for her guidance, her wisdom, and her counsel. I am also incredibly grateful for my editor, Nina Rodríguez-Marty, senior editor at Penguin Life. I speak on capitalism in this book, and hustle culture, and never once did I feel that "heat" from her. Nina always met me with compassion and not once was I asked to work past my limits—if anything I had to challenge my own internalized hustle and grind, as we all know I can turn on my Fight and tap out of my body cues quite well! My sincerest gratitude to Jan Baumer and Lauren Hall, my literary agents from Folio Literary Agency, as they have quite literally held my hands through this process and allowed this to be fun. Thank you for letting me heal and find joy in this journey. Julie Gallagher, you ray of sunshine, may the universe bless you for sticking by my side when we were working for the future, I love you! A special thank you to the rest of the publishing team, my media team, editing team, marketing team, and the entire force behind this magical book, as it would not be without your efforts that this book would be in its final form.

To my family, Mom, Dad, Tess, and Claire, thank you for always being there since day one. You were all a part of this book; in every story your essence was there and I know how lucky I am to have best friends in all of you! Thank you for always being a phone call away, or hopping on a flight whenever we need you—I am quite literally the luckiest middle child alive.

Sean, you are my rock, my best friend, and you watched me crumble and build back up again as I wrote this book. Thank you. Thank you for your patience, for the continued work that you do, for the laughter and joy you bring into this world, and for your companionship.

I also want to extend my gratitude to my therapists, health-care teams, and providers over the years who have heard me, believed me, and listened to me. To the nurses and anesthesiologists who have cared for me and not treated me as a number, thank you. To my neurosurgeon, we have been through it together, and I am so grateful for you, and to be under your care; thank you for seeing me, thank you for taking me seriously and believing me.

To the communities that continue to show up for their neighbors in need, thank you. To support groups and systems that are put into place by groups within our own communities that make it more accessible for us to heal from Body Grief, thank you. Individualism is burning out and the power of community is growing stronger because of you.

To the leaders within the anti-racism and anti-ableism movement, thank you. As a student I am beyond grateful; I am learning and growing and imperfectly in the work. I acknowledge your labor and hold space for the Body Grief that comes with that. Thank you.

Index